REALITY
Parenting

AS NOT SEEN ON
TV

TREION MULLER

AUTHOR OF **DAD RULES** AND CO-AUTHOR OF **MOM RULES**

D1706368

PLAIN SIGHT PUBLISHING

AN IMPRINT OF CEDAR FORT, INC.
SPRINGVILLE, UT

ISBN 13: 978-1-4621-1397-2

Published by Plain Sight Publishing, an imprint of Cedar Fort, Inc.
2373 W. 700 S., Springville, UT 84663
Distributed by Cedar Fort, Inc., www.cedarfort.com

LIBRARY OF CONGRESS CATALOGING-IN-PUBLICATION DATA

Muller, Treion, 1972- author.
Reality parenting / Treion Muller.
    pages cm
Includes bibliographical references and index.
Summary: Addresses topics such as "terrible twos," "toddler tantrums," family trips, school stuff, being a soccer parent, and the everyday madness that comes with parenthood.
ISBN 978-1-4621-1397-2 (alk. paper)
1. Child rearing. 2. Parenthood. I. Title.
HQ769.M92746 2014
649'.1--dc23
                                    2013045698

Cover design by Angela D. Baxter
Cover design © 2014 by Lyle Mortimer
Edited and typeset by Whitney Lindsley

Printed in the United States of America

10 9 8 7 6 5 4 3 2 1

THIS BOOK IS DEDICATED TO ALL THE
REAL MOMS AND DADS WHO DO THE BEST
THEY CAN EVERY DAY.

PRAISE FOR
REALITY PARENTING

"The table of contents in Treion Muller's *Reality Parenting* may look like a joke set list at a comedy club, but even though he uses humor to communicate his message, the 'reality' is he deals with serious issues that he backs up with facts, experiences, solutions, and an opportunity for self examination. It's a fun read but there's never TMI when it comes to the real work of parenting exposed inside his latest book."

—Bruce R. Hough, president of Nutraceutical, father of 10, and grandfather of 16, and counting . . .

"Front-line challenges deserve front-line realism. Thank you, Treion Muller, for restoring humor, entertainment, and realism to the wonderful world of parenting. Brilliant, simply brilliant!"

—Marlaine Cover, bestselling author of *Kissing the Mirror*, founder of Parenting 2.0, and creator of the Life Skills Report Card

"*Reality Parenting* is a light and humorous journey through the ups and downs of the average parent. A journey that will keep you smiling as you relate to the misadventures of the real families whose stories are woven into the fabric of the many universal principles being taught."

—Hyrum W. Smith, bestselling author of *What Matters Most* and cofounder and former CEO of FranklinCovey

"Treion Muller understands today's parenting struggles, and presents scenarios in a wise, but humorous way. Reality Parenting will encourage parents, while offering them solid suggestions for reflection and improvement."

—Cheri J. Meiners, author of the Learning to Get Along and Being the Best Me children's series

"*Reality Parenting* made me realize I'm not alone in feeling the chaos around parenting two girls! Treion made me laugh, reflect, and taught me some new text speak I didn't know existed! *Reality Parenting* is a must-read for parents seeking to give their children their best while balancing career, community involvement, and getting things done."

—Dr. Rollan Roberts II, CEO, TV Personality, and author of *Born to Be Rich*

"Someone finally did it! Created an excellent handbook on how to be a great parent. Treion has managed to create a humorous, practical, and principle-based approach to everyday parenting. My wife and I will use it wisely. I encourage everyone to do the same."

—Sam Bracken, author of *My Orange Duffel Bag: A Journey to Radical Change* and *Unwind: 7 Paradigms of a Stress Free Life*

CONTENTS

IMPERFECTLY FINE

DON'T DIS THE "FUNCTIONAL" IN YOUR
   DYSFUNCTIONAL

YOU ARE A SURVIVOR

REALITY SELF-ASSESSMENT

THERE IS NO PAUSE BUTTON

WHAT GOES AROUND COMES AROUND

RESPECT YOUR WINGMAN (OR WOMAN)

UNSPORTSMANLIKE CONDUCT

SOMETIMES YOU JUST CAN'T WIN

HELP IS ON THE WAY

P.S. YOU'LL NEVER "ARRIVE"

CHILDBIRTH (FROM HIS AND HER
   PERSPECTIVE)

PARENTAL AGORAPHOBIA

THE SHINY OBJECT TRICK

DON'T FORGET THE POTTY!

PARENTING CAN BE A BLOODY MESS

THE TEMPORARY ORPHAN PARENTING
   TECHNIQUE

ACKNOWLEDGMENTS & CONTRIBUTIONS

THIS BOOK IS A COMPILATION OF REALITIES, PRINciples, and real-life stories that has been brought to life through many wonderful contributions by parents like you. In order to respect the privacy of these parents and their children, and in many cases save them from embarrassment, I have changed the names of people in all the stories found in the book. But I would like to recognize their great contributions by putting their names in this section. So if you see your name, chances are your story, thoughtful quote, or inspirational example can be found in the book. Thank you!

First, a major shout-out to Alex Herzog and Emily Ballard for their great contributions to this book! Your stories, ideas, and wit have inspired me and will inspire those who read the book. I would also like to thank Sean Covey for a wonderful foreword.

Thank you to the following parents and their children who have added their personal touch throughout the book (in no specific order): Dennis Gibbons, Spencer and Kimberly Mordue, Yvonne van Dijk, Yvonne Theron, Sam Bracken, Judy Ball, Marius Von Mollendorf, Courtney and Dave Fuller, Whitney Permann,

Brooke Stone, Breck England, James Keddington, Gregory Bland, Allison Mayoros, Becky and Shannen Kelly, Tarren Youlten, Catherine and Wade Reed, Mindy Olsen, Faith Freeman, Nikki and Roberto De Carvalo, Brad and Mandi Augustin, Josh Covey, Julee Mobley, Zach Adams, Karen and Steve Mordue, Jody Karr, John Hilton III, Kip and Stacey Willis, Rachel Gifford-Sidaway, Barbara and Boyd Mordue, Sheridan Mordue, Ryan Christiansen, and Josh and Suz Eaton.

Also, a big thanks to my Parenting 2.0 LinkedIn colleagues, family professionals, and fellow ambassadors for your stories, advice, and influence: Marlaine Cover, Sharon Neely, Michelle Hutchinson, Avram Baskin, Tom Krause, Tamera Young, Norman Cooper, Ray Erickson, Rodney Davis, Malika Bourne, Annie Fox, Leah Davis, Donna Volpitta, Anthea Thomas, Anand Pajpani, Rosalind Cutler, Lynne Kenney, Dennis A. Daniel, Marji Zintz, Wendy Wolff, Erwin and Jane Kaufman, Gary Screaton, Madeline Binder, Michelle Turan, Melissa Pazan, Robin Schafer, Dennis Sheridan, Madeline Binder, Patricia Porter, and Tommy Maloney.

Most of all thanks to my wife, Soni, who may not be a perfect parent but is mighty close. And to my five amazing children who have colored my life with humor, drama, and thousands of small moments. I love you.

FOREWORD
BY SEAN COVEY

MOST OF US DEAL PRETTY WELL WITH REALITY from day to day. Then we become parents. This is a new reality weirder than any reality I could have ever fathomed. I like how Bill Cosby said it: "My wife and I were intellectuals. And then we had children."

In this reality, little people run around naked in public. They put cheeseburgers under the car seats. They throw up on you, bleed on you, and even poop on you—sometimes all at the same time. When they scream, you panic. When they go silent, you worry. And when they hug you, you cry.

This is a terrific little book, a wiki for parents who are clueless—which includes all parents. (By the way, before I had children, I used to make a lot of comments about what good parenting entails. Now that I have children, I too am clueless.) There's no theory here, just plain, sloppy, warm-your-heart reality. It just tells you the truth: you're going to need lots of bandages.

You'll learn a lot here—how to make a diaper with paper towels and duct tape, how to live happily in a barn that is also a pigsty, how to have "the talk" without making eye contact, how to use shiny objects to trick a small child into eating, and how to handle it when your four-year-old refers to your spouse as a twelve-letter obscenity.

I'm the father of eight children. (I can't believe it either. My wife and I never got the memo, I suppose.) So I need this book, and so do you. I need the timeless principles for turning the lunacy into lasting family love. I particularly need the wonderful guide to having "reality talks" with children, a wise and empathetic approach to getting close to your child's heart while healing it at the same time. The "reality check" questions are simple but deep—as you answer them for yourself, you'll discover that you already have unique gifts that a parent needs to succeed. You'll also discover that it's okay to make mistakes.

You'll learn **TXTSPK**—the alien language of texting, in which all children (aliens that they are) are fluent. Along with this digital dictionary, you'll also find fresh, basic advice on how to disconnect your kids from their phones long enough to make their acquaintance. Good luck on that one.

Best of all, you'll learn about being surprised, as when your son announces he no longer needs to shower ("I've taken enough of them, don't you think?") or your daughter won't put her shoes on "because I have a date with destiny." And you'll be surprised by love—overwhelming, blinding love.

In the last analysis, I believe there is nothing more important than family. And as you'll see in this book, there are no relationships more joyful and challenging and lasting than those with our children. Remember, on their deathbed, nobody wished they'd spent more time at the office.

So read this book, moms and dads. You need it, **FWIW**. And it's worth a lot.

HI, MY NAME IS TREION, AND I AM THE PROUD, THE perplexed, the permanently befuddled father of five children. Five! That's five unique personalities that require five different parenting approaches. I only know one, and it's not even a very good approach. In other words, I have a long way to go. However, I have made it my purpose in life to become a great dad even if takes a lifetime, which it may.

When I am not at work, I am driving in carpools; attending soccer games, recitals, and parent-teacher conferences; and doing much more kid "stuff." I don't have a lot of time for myself. My dear wife doesn't get a break either. She's the family CEO. Her days and nights are spent running our family business, the primary mission being to raise service-oriented, fully functional, responsible children. It is not easy, but we love our children, and this is the life we have chosen. This is our reality.

You might be surprised to hear this, but in many ways we are a dysfunctional family too. I don't know of any family that is perfect. If reality TV teaches us anything, it's that some families may look perfect on the outside, but underneath it all they are a mess. I wrote this book with my family in mind and to help other parents confront their realities, cope with the everyday, and generally to just survive the day-to-day. Which is why I would also like to invite you to share your parenting reality with me and the community by commenting at realityparentsrus.com.

So enjoy this realistic and humorous look inside my family and the dozens of other families whose stories are found in the pages of this book.

XOXO

"A child's life is like a piece of paper on which every passerby leaves a mark."
Chinese proverb

REALITY PARENTING

I F YOU ARE READING THIS, CHANCES ARE YOU ARE a parent or one to be—a mother or father whose life doesn't look anything like the "reality" television shows, movies, and books you've been introduced to. But this wasn't always the case.

Growing up in the seventies, eighties, and nineties, I watched family friendly shows like *The Cosby Show, Who's the Boss?, Growing Pains, Charles in Charge,* and *Family Ties.* There were no *Survivor* islands, Jersey shores, weight loss resorts, or camera crews following a bunch of spoiled celebrities around all day, every day. The shows I watched generally taught family values even if in short episodes and through exaggerated humor. There was safety in the consistent and quirky parenting style of parents like Dr. Huxtable (Bill Cosby) and Mrs. Keaton (from *Family Ties*), who parented with unconditional love and steady discipline. Parents who were always present in their children's lives. Every day. Every show.

Then things started to change. Hollywood started dishing up two extreme perspectives on a nightly sitcom basis when it came to family entertainment.

On one extreme, sitcom fathers are typified as spineless, philandering deadbeats unable to hold down a job or keep commitments,

1

while mothers in many of these shows are portrayed as uneducated, superficial divas who aren't able to care for themselves or their children. And according to contemporary programming, all children are spoiled, dysfunctional misfits who despise their parents. There are exceptions, but they are hard to find.

On the other extreme, family life is portrayed with the glitz, glamour, and paparazzi of a Kardashian reality show. In real life, most mothers can't afford a nanny to raise their children while they get daily massages, makeovers, and a personal trainer to help sculpt their buns into steel.

Yet, prime-time TV is where Americans spend their *prime* time; getting a snapshot into the life and follies of fictional families while laughing at their misadventures and dysfunctional lives. And this is how we, as a society, help proliferate skewed paradigms concerning what family life should look and feel like. It's time we awake from our hypnotic allegiance to the "tube," stop watching someone else's reality, and start living our own.

Fortunately, most real families are actually functioning relatively well despite our unique dysfunctions and *in spite* of the entertainment industry. Our reality can probably be more accurately defined as continuous chaos interrupted by rare moments of peace . . . usually when the kids are in bed.

Being a good mother or father is far from being glamorous and doesn't come with commercial breaks. It's unmade beds, endless laundry, exhausting days, and three-week-old leftovers in the fridge. It's pushing through to the weekend just to discover you actually don't have a weekend anymore; it's been sacrificed to the soccer, football, gymnastics, and dance gods.

This is reality parenting! And it has always been the reality. We just have to look away from the screen to find it.

Reality parenting is also the small kisses and unconditional hugs, the sweet memories and hundreds of "first times." It's those moments when you overflow with so much emotion that your eyes cannot contain it all. It's holding on tightly and knowing when to let go. It's smothering with love and allowing freedom to grow. It's hard to endure at times—and even harder to express—but like the millions who have gone on before you, it comes naturally. You just know what to do. This is reality parenting! The precious moments that cannot be felt or captured by reality TV, only in your heart and home.

While everyone's reality is a little different, we also have much in common. Since becoming a father, I look at parent–child interactions a lot differently. I used to judge other parents and take note of what I wouldn't do if I were in their situation. I am ashamed of my pre-parental self-righteousness. Reality has humbled me. What before was a noisy brat at the grocery store is now just a child testing his boundaries. I no longer hear crying babies in airplanes, just the sweet music of heaven in a frustrated infant's melody. And I feel for the mom or dad who is picking up the cereal boxes his screaming child has dumped in the grocery store aisle. Yes, as parents we continue to grow and learn just like our kids.

Reality Parenting is my attempt to share what I have learned from raising five children in a reality world without cameras or scripts. It is my candid and honest opinion on parenting—the good, the bad, and the ugly. The five core principles underlying every chapter in this book are

1. **Imperfection.** My first goal is to help parents understand that *there are no perfect parents*, no perfect families, just imperfect "parents in motion" that are hoping they can survive the day. The reality is that we have a better

chance of surviving if we can help one another, learn from one another, and share what we learn in return—not judge one another. This is the new parenting reality. We are all reality parents who would benefit by having helpful tips and insights on how to survive the everyday challenges that our families throw up.

2. **Survival.** *Reality Parenting* is for both the über-efficient and the "I just want to make it through today" parents. Think of it as a *survival guide*, and, like you would use any survival guide, be selective in what you take from it. Not every piece of advice is appropriate or relevant for you and your present circumstance.

3. **Preparation.** This book is also to help parents *be better prepared*. Although the Boy Scouts of America claim "Be Prepared" as their motto, these two words should become the catchphrase for parents worldwide because preparation is the only way to truly survive raising children. Even then you cannot be prepared for every potential adventure your offspring will get you into. It's having books to read or color at a moment's notice when the waiting room pushes the limits of time and space. It's about being mentally prepared for the questions and tenacious, investigative nature of a four-year-old and her many questions. It's about saving time, reducing stress, and being more in control. It's not designed to spoil spontaneity or creativity, merely to suggest that being more prepared will free you up to enjoy life and your kids more.

4. **Awareness.** Most of the reality parenting principles in this book are *not* intended to be a "one size fits all"

solution but are rather intended to raise your *aware-ness* regarding a parenting principle you may not have thought about or that you now think differently about. My hope is that your new awareness will inspire you to act or parent differently because only you can take some actions because of your unique parenting situation. After all, your reality is not my reality. The principles I need to work on and behaviors I need to change will be different than yours. We have different life skills and life challenges, but thankfully we also have many similarities.

5. **Improvement.** While you may not be perfect, you can still work at being a better father or mother than you were yesterday. This takes work, everyday attention, ongoing self-evaluation, and frequent adjustments: a "one thing at a time" type of focus. Remember, the only way you'll eat this humongous elephant is by one small, incremental, seemingly insignificant bite at a time.

The remainder of the book is a compilation of parenting rules, tips, real-life applications, and parenting realities. It is not an exhaustive list by any means, just a sampling. You will also find "Reality Checks" throughout the book that will give you the opportunity to self-reflect, self-evaluate, and assess your current status with regards to the many reality parenting principles you will read about. If you take advantage of these checks and act upon your own introspections, you will see significant progress as a person and a parent.

Now, as you dive into the principles and stories that follow, I hope you will find a few relevant parenting nuggets that will help you with your very own custom-made parenting reality.

TXTSPK CRASH COURSE

SINCE YOU'RE READING A BOOK ON PARENTING, why not also take a crash course on the new language your kids are using at the same time? It's called "text speak," and it's mostly spoken with their thumbs . . . on their cell phones. Yes, texting is a new language that all parents need to learn if they truly wish to communicate with, or at least understand, their children.

With this intent in mind, I have included **TXTSPK** (text speak) throughout the book along with the regular, boring definition of the word or phrase in "PARENTheses" for parents.

BTW (by the way), I have not written the whole book in this new language. That wouldn't be a good idea. Even these last few sentences are more text speak than you'll typically see in the remainder of the book.

Oh, and there will be a test at the end of the book. Seriously, there is. But it also comes with the answer key, so don't stress about it.

YW (You're welcome.)

1. CONFRONTING YOUR REALITY

IMPERFECTLY FINE

Being the author of parenting books—*Dad Rules: A Simple Manual for a Complex Job* and *Mom Rules: Because Even Superheroes Need Help Sometimes*—I have really set myself up for criticism. For example, over the past couple of years, my mother-in-law has suggested I read my own book. I had a nephew sit on a couch during a family gathering, read my book, and occasionally point at me and laugh. And my own offspring have reminded me on several occasions of the rules I was breaking. **WTH** (What the heck)?

In my defense, I have never claimed perfection in any of my books. Quite the opposite, actually. I always include a disclaimer (like I did in this book) stating that I am an imperfect father in motion and that I have written these parenting books to help me as much as anyone else.

Actually, one of the motivating factors for writing *Reality Parenting* came from a seemingly insignificant event several years ago that involved the TV, an imperfect father (me), and an inspired wife.

Like many people today, I would spend hours each night mesmerized by the magic box (it was still a box then). Losing myself in the thrill of the game or the latest plot or obscure and fascinating characters. It was easy to be sucked into a good story line, and before I knew it, another "season" and year was gone. Sadly, while I was watching other people's fake lives, my own life was passing by without me in it. My children were getting older, and I had lost quality time with them that I could never get back. In retrospect, I was quite pathetic as a parent.

Thankfully, my wise and patient wife pulled me from the addicting clutches of the entertainment world before I wasted more time away from what matters most, my family.

It was at that time that we decided to turn off the TV and be present in body and spirit with our children and one another. I believe this decision saved our family. I think of it as an inspired awakening from being in a TV-induced coma.

Honestly, I didn't think I had a problem. I was only watching TV at night, and I wasn't watching what was considered to be "bad" programming. I rationalized that since it was acceptable material to watch, it was okay for me to watch it. However, after extracting myself from the situation, I realized that anything that distracted me from my family was bad programming.

Not all television is bad . . . we will still watch certain television shows and movies, but we do so in moderation. The point is not to suggest that all entertainment is evil, but rather to warn parents of the dangers of excessive viewing habits and the harmful effects it can have on quality family time.

Our nights are now spent doing homework with the kids, driving them to extracurricular activities, and participating in activities they enjoy (which sometimes includes watching a movie). After we put our children to bed at night, instead of picking up the remote control, we pick up a good book and read (or write about our parenting adventures, of course).

So the next time you reach for that remote control, think of it as a time machine that will shoot you forward in time without the option to come back. Then remember that turning that magical box off saved my family and rescued me from living with regret. I can promise you that doing the same in your home will only yield positive results.

The reality is that you and I are not perfect, and neither are those parents who live down the street from you who you think are perfect. Ironically, they are probably stumbling along their own parenting path and looking to you for examples of good parenting. But we are all working really hard on being better.

Take a deep breath and give yourself a break. Walk away from the edge and remember you are not perfect. You will never be a perfect parent. Being imperfect is perfectly fine.

DON'T DIS THE "FUNCTIONAL" IN YOUR DYSFUNCTIONAL

The good news is that there is always some level of functional in every dysfunctional family. Look for it. Find it. Hold fast to it, whatever *it* is. Your functional could be knowing how to calmly deal with the madness around you or finding humor in the humorless, like the following declaration of imperfection from a real mother our family knows well:

"Spent yesterday canning applesauce. Stevie decided it was a good time to throw up every few hours, which by the end of the day was straight applesauce. Before bed I noticed some applesauce in my hair, but I wasn't sure *which* applesauce it was. I nominated myself for 'The Most Awesome Mother Ever Who Juggles

Applesauce *and* a Vomiting Cranky Toddler' award (it's quite prestigious). And then I showered."

I was seriously **ROFL** (rolling on the floor laughing) when I first read this. Like this mom, sometimes we need to look for the one thing we are doing well and hold on to it, even if everything else is falling apart around us. In your parenting battles do not give up the ground you have already won. Arthur Ashe, American World number-one professional tennis player, said it best: "Start where you are. Use what you have. Do what you can."

IMHO (in my humble opinion), there are no functional families, just some who are less dysfunctional.

If you, like my dear wife, are one of those parents who compares yourself to other mothers or fathers, I would highly recommend reading, *The Gifts of Imperfection* by Brene Brown.[1] This delightful book helps us self-inflicted perfectionists make the transition from "What will people think?" to "I am good enough."

REALITY CHECK

MY ROAD TO PERFECTION EXERCISE

1. List all the things you are doing well. (Examples— you do dinner together . . . most nights; you read bedtime stories . . . most of the time; you have frequent chats with your kids . . . sometimes; you're a good listener . . . occasionally.)

2. List some of the things you feel you want to be doing better as a parent and as a family.

3. Circle just one or two behaviors from your list under #2.

4. Identify how you plan to start acting on these identified behaviors.

5. Plan when you will start. For example, family dinner together. Determine when your family can realistically all get together. Write it down.

6. Share your goal with your family.

7. Stick to it.

8. Once you are habitually performing your new behaviors, select new ones from your list and repeat steps 3 through 7.

9. Repeat until you have mastered all of those behaviors you have identified, and then start again.

LESS FORMAL OPTION:

Think of one or two things you want to do better and make it happen. Then work on another, and another, until you die still an imperfect (but improved) human being.

YOU ARE A SURVIVOR

Forget about being stranded on an uninhabitable island with a group of strangers and little to no food. The real survivors are parents.

And since most parenting takes place in the day-to-day rituals and everyday madness, this would be a good place to start honing your survival skills. Regardless of how many children you have or what you do for a living, chances are your daily routine can be quite hectic and unmanageable at times. Even though your reality may be very different from mine, see if you can relate to my daily routine.

My typical day as a husband and father:

A typical day for me starts with the annoying sound of an alarm at 5:00 a.m. so that I can exercise before eating breakfast with the family and racing off to work. After an exhausting day at the office, I drive home just to get back in the car again to take one of the kids to gymnastics or dance or soccer. On the way home *again*, I receive a text from my wife to pick up some essentials at the grocery store. After shoving dinner down my throat, I am on the road again to pick up aforementioned kids from aforementioned activities. And then I return home for a third time just in time to help my wife brush kids' teeth, put jammies on, and sprint through a story before saying kiddie prayers. I finally collapse on my bed and force myself to stay awake so I can catch up with my lovely wife for the first time in the day.

My wife's typical day as a mother:

I wake up to my husband's annoying alarm clock at 5:00 a.m., and I can never fall back to sleep, so I get up and make five different breakfasts for five different kids. After pushing most of the kids out the door in time for school, I spend the rest of the day trying to entertain a two- and four-year-old and get them down for naps so I can do the laundry, wash the dishes, and clean the house. When the older kids are back home from school, we tackle homework and piano practice before my husband has to take them to gymnastics or dance or soccer. In between homework and piano, I attempt to make a semi-healthy dinner before my husband has to pick the kids up from their activities. After dinner, I clear up the dinner table and get the younger kids ready for bed. Then I remember that we are don't have milk for tomorrow, which would be a breakfast disaster, so I text the hubby to pick up the milk and a loaf of bread at the store on his way home from picking the kids up. Getting everyone's teeth brushed and jammies on takes longer than it should, and story time and prayers are usually rushed. This is all before I collapse on my bed and force myself to stay awake so that I can catch up with my handsome husband for the first time in the day.

While this is reality parenting, there are some things you can do to survive each day. Start by looking at yourself in mirror every morning and reciting: *My name is _____, and I will survive today!*

Then get to work, because as you know, there are no production teams, makeup artists, or teleprompters to tell you what you should do or say. And if you don't show up for your daily curtain call, no one will, and that just isn't a viable option.

REALITY SELF-ASSESSMENT

You know you are a reality parent if you have ever . . .

(Check all that apply, add up your check marks, and then read the corresponding key.)

- ☐ Wanted to go on an overnight "romantic" getaway just so you could catch up on sleep.

☐ Forgotten to pick up your child from school or another activity.

☐ Thought of moving to a foreign country or desolate island without letting anyone know.

☐ Been far from home without diapers or wipes or pacifiers or bottles when you've needed them the most.

☐ Used your children's toothbrush because you couldn't find yours.

☐ Looked forward to going to work because it felt like a vacation away from home.

☐ Visited a local fast food joint so often you are on a first name basis with the employees.

☐ Forgotten the name(s) of one or more of your children.

☐ Lost one of your children in a public place.

☐ Gone weeks without a good night's rest.

☐ Ran out of toilet paper and used paper towels or wipes instead.

☐ Even though you've both been living under the same roof and sleeping in the same bed, you've gone days without speaking to your spouse because you've been so busy with kid stuff.

☐ Put on the TV (or a movie) for your kids so you can get stuff done.

☐ Run out of clean clothes because you were too busy to do laundry.

☐ Done a head count to make sure everyone is accounted for.

☐ Fallen asleep at your work desk, on your living room floor, or at another unconventional place at random times in the day.

☐ Been so busy you have forgotten to bathe your children for a week.

☐ Gone without bathing yourself for a few days.

☐ Not wanted to go on vacation with your children because it's more work than vacation.

Key:

1–6 : Chances are your kids are still young or they have left home. Good luck it's going to get harder OR congratulations you survived, depending on which category you fall under.

7–12 : Things are still manageable but they are starting to get crazy.

13–19 : You are in the day-to-day of reality parenting. Good luck!

THERE IS NO PAUSE BUTTON

Besides all of the day-to-day madness, you will have times when you just want to press pause and say, "Hold on for just a minute! Let me gather my thoughts together and figure out what to do. I just need time to think and catch up with everything that's going on."

The following introspective monologue is an example of those moments in our lives when we realize that time has passed without us knowing it. I call these moments "searching for the pause button."

"How in the world did Andrew grow out of his church shoes already? They're only a few weeks old. His white shirt is already too short for him, and he still needs a haircut. And speaking of haircuts, has it already been a solid eighteen months since I've had a haircut? Andie is upset because she thought I shrunk her new dress. It's polyester. And I washed it in cold and hung flat to dry, so I don't think that's even possible. It must also be too small already."

Unfortunately, life has no pause button, which means experiences, opportunities, and memories sometimes slip past us before we can enjoy them.

I sometimes still think of my oldest daughter, Chloe, as the cute and cuddly toddler who adored her daddy, sat on his lap, and ran to me, arms outstretched, to me when I came home from work. Sadly, that little girl is gone forever; I will never see her again. In her place is a beautiful, smart, and vibrant young lady who is almost as tall as me and who luckily still likes her daddy . . . at least most of the time.

The reality is that a lot of inches, memories, and parenting has taken place between the younger and the older Chloe but seemingly not a lot of time. Time is the premium currency here, and I often find myself searching for the pause button as well.

In both of my previous parenting books (*Dad Rules* and *Mom Rules*), the first rule is "show up for the job every day." Following this rule helps parents be present in their children's lives and enjoy the time they do have with them before it is too late—before they have regrets of missing their children grow up.

Another practice all parents can adopt in order to cherish the present is to keep a journal or blog. I know not everyone loves writing as much as I do, but it doesn't have to be anything fancy. Just the act of writing down what you have observed in your family every day (or as often as you can) helps you be more aware and stay in the moment. I have a blog (theboogerblog.com) that is made up of short posts reflecting my day-to-day reality. Nothing special, yet very special to me and, I hope, to my family one day.

PRESS PAUSE—CREATE A FAMILY MASTERPIECE

Here is a family-friendly activity that may not pause life, but it will at least allow you to capture a small moment in time. It started several years ago while I was painting a still life for fun and relaxation. Since there was paper and paint and brushes involved, my young children wanted to participate as well. At first I resisted, not wanting my relaxation to be turned into chaos and for my little ones to create an inevitable mess. Then I saw an opportunity to do something together as a family. Here are the steps we followed in creating our first family masterpiece. Give it a try.

1. Take a large piece of thick paper or canvas and spread it out on a table.

2. Place paints of all colors around the canvas and give everyone in the family a paintbrush.

3. Decide as a family what you'll paint. Keep your topic or theme simple, like a family garden or fruit.

4. Explain that there are no rules, no limits, no lines, and no rush.

5. Everyone starts painting together on the same canvas.

6. Add glue, glitter, and other stuff if you want.

7. No matter how it ends up, frame it and hang it on a wall somewhere in your house for all to see.

8. Repeat every year.

WHAT GOES AROUND COMES AROUND

A couple of summers ago, I was coasting in a speedboat with my teenage nephew Jake at Lake Powell. As we approached the marina, I saw a houseboat full of beautiful bronzed women—and a wonderful opportunity to embarrass Jake.

As we were passing the party boat, Uncle Treion decided it was time to show his young nephew how *not* to impress women. Think of it as a lesson in what not to do. With a Diet Coke in one hand and another hand on the steering wheel of the boat, I put on my best *Nacho Libre* impression and yelled, "Hello, pretty ladies!" Two things happened: Jake went bright red and hid his face, and the pretty ladies all looked at me in disgust (I know they were thinking "dirty old man"). I had achieved my goal.

Now fast-forward to 2013. My very own boy, barely two years old, turned to his sisters at breakfast one day and said, "Hello, pretty ladies!" We were all shocked. I had not used that phrase since my attempt at humor at Lake Powell. Come to find out that Jake, while embarrassed at the time, thought the experience was rather funny and shared it with all his friends, and they all started using the phrase as a joke with their girl friends. Well, in the process, Jake's younger brother also picked up the expression and in turn taught it to my boy.

What left my mouth as a joke intended for one person returned to my ears from the lips of my Don Juan son.

James Baldwin, the American novelist, essayist, playwright, and poet, taught this parenting reality perfectly when he said, "Children have never been good at listening to their elders, but they have never failed to imitate them." And according to several studies conducted by Albert Bandura regarding social learning theory, children tend to imitate their adult role models especially when it came to aggressive behaviors.[2]

The lesson I have learned from this experience is that parenting is a full-time job, and what you do and say impacts your children more than you think.

Yep, what goes around comes around . . . especially if you are a parent.

REALITY CHECK

WHAT MAY COME BACK AROUND?

Besides the words you use, what other behaviors or choices are you making that could come back to haunt you?

RESPECT YOUR WINGMAN (OR WOMAN)

How many times have you said "no" to something just to have that child return with, "But Dad, Mom said it was okay!"

If it's something I feel strongly about, I will ask my wife if she was aware that I said no. Most of the time it is not, and had she known, she would have said no too, even if she didn't feel as strongly about it. And visa versa. We then enact our parental executive veto powers and undo the previous decision and have a talk with the offending parties about the meaning of "no." However, there are times when your wingman (or woman) may be correct in their opposing decision, and you should apologize to your children and admit that you may have been rash in what you said. Mom and Dad Rule #38 is "When you mess up, say, 'I'm sorry.'"

Either way, respect your other half's decisions. Be sure to counsel together on how to approach sensitive subjects with your children and be in agreement on the appropriate actions to take before you find yourself in the situation. Most of all, you need to have your spouse's back, and he or she needs to have yours. And if you feel he or she is wrong on a specific point, then talk to him or her in private about it, not in front of the kiddos.

This is only way to survive the parental trap of being attacked on several fronts by cunning children who have learned the deadly art of manipulation through knowing your weaknesses.

REALITY CHECK

SINGLE-PARENT REALITY CHECK

If you are "winging it" on your own, then find someone else to be your wingman/woman—perhaps your child's aunt, uncle, grandparent, or even a family friend. Someone you completely trust to support you and your decisions and to help you talk through any mistakes you may have made. If you are wrong, it's your responsibility to admit it to your child.

UNSPORTSMANLIKE CONDUCT

Unsportsmanlike conduct should never be called on a parent who is sitting on the sidelines watching a game, but unfortunately some parents still don't know how to behave in public. I'm as competitive and volatile as the next dad, but whenever I get the urge to yell at an umpire or referee, I stop and say to myself, "Treion, it's only a game. Don't say anything stupid that will embarrass you or your child." Most of the time this little pep talk does the trick.

Even when the mom on the bleachers next to you is yelling at your son or daughter, tell yourself she is just a crazy lady who can't help herself and smile while you count to one hundred . . . very slowly.

To address the challenge of super-involved parents at kids' sporting events, the city of Buffalo Grove, Illinois, decided to put up the following sign:

> *Things for coaches, parents, and spectators to keep in mind while children are playing sports on our field:*
> *This is a* game *being played by* children.
>
> *If they win or lose every game of the season, it will not impact what college they attend or their future income potential.*
>
> *Of the hundreds of thousands of children who have ever played youth sports in Buffalo Grove, very few have gone on to play professionally. It is highly unlikely that any college recruiters or professional scouts are watching these games, so let's keep it all about having fun and being pressure-free.*
>
> *Imagine how you would feel if you saw a parent or coach from the opposing team cheering for your child when they made a great play. Then envision what kind of person you would think they are for doing that. You can be that person.*
>
> *Referees, umpires, and officials are human and make mistakes, just like players, coaches, and you. No one shouts at you in front of other people when you make a mistake, so please don't yell at them. We do not have video replay, so we will go with their calls.*
>
> *The only reason children want to play sports is because it is fun. Please don't let the behavior of adults ruin their fun.*[3]

While there are some who criticized the city for putting up the signs, I tip my hat to them for having the courage to take a stand to protect kids from their own parents and people like me just waiting to explode.

REALITY CHECK

AM I A GOOD SPORT?

Since you may not be completely honest with yourself on this reality check, you may want to ask these questions of someone who will be honest with you, like your sports-playing child or your spouse. If these members of your family are like mine, they will be extremely honest.

1. Do I yell too much at your games?

2. Is it okay if I yell encouraging words to you and your teammates?

3. What else would you like me to stop doing at your games?

4. What would you like me to start doing at your games?

SOMETIMES YOU JUST CAN'T WIN

A friend, pastor, and fellow parenting author shared an experience that shows how, even when you do everything right as a parent, sometimes things can still go very wrong:

"When our daughters were younger and beginning school, Leanne and I decided we should teach them about appropriate and inappropriate touch. In our minds, 'street proofing' our children felt like the right thing to do. We approached the topic with care and compassion, wanting to make them wise without violating their innocence.

"Several weeks later, we were walking through a local mall. As we did so, Katie, my oldest daughter (five years old at the time), picked up on a game we typically played. We would hold hands, and she would run, jump, and swing up in the air and land flat on her back cradled in my arms. It was a lot of fun for both of us. On her last run, swing, and jump, she landed cradled in my arms with her shirt slightly raised, exposing her belly. In that moment, I bent my head forward (as I had done since the day she was born) and placed my lips on her belly and blew.

"Normally this would immediately result in giggles and laughter. Not today. Instead she screamed a horrific blood-curdling scream that could be heard above all the noise and chatter in the mall: 'DON'T TOUCH ME THERE!' Not once, not twice, but three times I heard, 'DON'T TOUCH ME THERE.' She was doing exactly at we had taught her to do, but obviously we had failed to reinforce what appropriate touch was.

"Mortified at what I was hearing, I froze, stopped blowing on her tummy, and hesitantly looked up. It was like a scene out of *The Matrix*. Everything was moving in slow motion. As I glanced to the left and to the right, I came in contact with the steely, cold stares of several women who had come to the aid of my child.

"In that moment, all of my developmental psychology training flooded my mind, and I remembered that children are concrete thinkers . . . and that I had some explaining to do."

Moms and dads, sometimes we can't do anything else but throw up our hands and laugh because in some cases there is nothing we could have done differently.

HELP IS ON THE WAY

No matter how strong or independent you are, there are moments in your life as a parent that you will need help.

IRL (In real life) asking for help is not a sign of weakness; it's actually a very smart thing to do if you want to survive parenthood.

This piece of advice is not just for you **NOOBS** (new parents but also means new at anything). It's for you seasoned vets too. Yes, you, the mom or dad of three teenage kids. This is the first and foremost tip I will offer because sometimes you just can't do it alone.

My wife, Soni, was recently in the recording studio laying down a new album, I was working long hours at the office, and the kids still needed be chauffeured to gymnastics and piano and soccer. That week we could not do it alone, and we needed help. We don't like to inconvenience or "put people out," so it was hard to ask for help, but we did. Our neighbors gladly stepped up and helped shuffle our children around so that we didn't have to stress about everything that we needed to do at home.

Asking for help may be especially hard for men, who may have been raised to be tough, to fix it up ourselves, and if we can't fix it, we use duct tape to hold it together. Well, duct tape cannot hold everything together, especially families.

When it comes to asking for help, don't forget divine intervention.

Sometimes believing in a power bigger than us, no matter what or who that power is, can be a source of strength and hope to parents. Some turn to prayer, meditation, worship, faith, contemplation, or pondering. Seeking divine instruction and help has been around for as long as we have recorded history. With such a large body of work supporting the practice of turning to a superior being for help in times of need, there must be something to it.

I know that when I have found myself in a bind without another human to call on for help, I have always found solace and peace in turning to my God—especially when I am at my wits' end with my kids and don't know what else to do. I just raise my thoughts heavenward and ask for help. It usually comes in the form of a thought and a peaceful feeling.

There is also a very advantageous side effect when you routinely turn to a higher source for help—your children learn from you that it is okay to ask for help and that all humans are vulnerable at times.

REALITY CHECK

HELP

1. Who can I turn to for questions and help?

2. How often during the week do I turn to spiritual guidance and reflection?

P.S. YOU'LL NEVER "ARRIVE"

We have already established that you are not a perfect parent and that you will never be one. **JSYK** (just so you know), there is also no "happy place" where parents go when they have passed all of the parenting tests, where they are greeted by parenting all-stars and showered with confetti and praise. No, you don't just wake up one day having arrived. You just get back in the saddle and go to work—hopefully doing a better job today than you did the day before.

However, I have been informed that there is a loophole to this reality—according to those who know, you've arrived once you become a grandparent. You still may not be perfect, but the arrangement is perfect. Based on the many conversations I have had with grandparents, adding "grand" to your title changes the game dramatically. While they love their grandchildren and worry about them as much as they did their own children, grandparents also enjoy the fact that they can send them home with their parents at the end of the day. I think this would be the perfect arrangement too. It gives you just enough time to recover and do your own thing and not worry about what the little people want to do all the time.

However, until you reach that "grand" status, you and I still have a lot of work to do and a lot of realities to face. I'll see you fellow warriors on the front lines.

NOTES

1. Brene Brown, *The Gifts of Imperfection* (Center City, MN: Hazelden Publishing, 2010).

2. A. Bandura, "Influence of Models' Reinforcement Contingencies on the Acquisition of Imitative Responses," *Journal of Personality and Social Psychology* no. 1 (1965).

3. Buffalo Grove Park District sign, in "Simmer Down, Signs Tell Sporting Parents," *Chicago Tribune* online, June 3, 2013, http://articles.chicagotribune.com/2013-06-03/news/ct-talk-playground-rules-20130603_1_signs-college-recruiters-parents.

2. THE REALITY OF PARENTING BABIES & TODDLERS

CHILDBIRTH

Before we progress any further into this reality parenting journey, let's take a moment to remember that unforgettable event that officially crowned us all mothers and fathers—childbirth. While adoption is just as momentous an occasion for mothers and fathers, this chapter focuses on the physical birthing of a child and not so much on becoming a parent.

Because men and women have such differing opinions and thoughts regarding this rather dramatic event, and every other parenting event for that matter, we are going to look at childbirth from his and her perspective.

From His Perspective

Men, take the time to learn about childbirth before you actually experience it in person. Childbirth is a life-changing event. It can also be very traumatic for dads. One minute it is just you and your wife, and the next minute there is a whole other person you are responsible for. No warning, just *BAM*! Congratulations, you are a daddy now. And no, that cigar or cheesy gift does not a daddy make. If anything, it brands him as another clueless man who has no idea what he has gotten himself into.

New dads have to be warned about childbirth because they typically have no idea what they are about to experience. Mothers go through birthing classes, read books about the experience, and receive instruction from their mothers or other women. They know what to expect when they are expecting. Not dads, or at least not me.

When I first entered the maternity ward thirteen years ago for the birth of our first child, I thought there might be some pushing and a little crying before we were handed a beautiful baby girl. Boy, was I wrong. I will never trust television shows anymore. Thanks to Hollywood, I thought babies were born in sixty minutes or less and that moms never broke a sweat or experienced much pain. Nope. Instead I was introduced to a real-life horror movie with blood and everything. And when I first heard Soni, my normally soft-spoken wife, scream like I had never heard her scream before, I knew I was in for a rude awakening.

It was also about this time that I went into a "man daze," or shock, and just went through the motions for the next few hours. While I was physically present by my wife's side as she went through waves of excruciating pain, I am ashamed to say I was probably not there mentally. However, that all changed the moment my baby girl made her grand entrance into the world. I thankfully awoke from my daze and witnessed the miracle of childbirth.

I have heard it said many times that nothing can prepare you for childbirth. Don't believe this age-old advice. You can do many things to prepare you for the growing event that officially designates you as a daddy.

1. For starters, read whatever your wife is reading. It may be geared toward the expectant mother, but the expecting daddy can learn a lot from those same books.

2. Talk to your wife in detail about what she expects will happen during childbirth and make sure you are on the same page. By the way, work on a backup plan with her in case she changes her mind during the event, especially with regards to pain medications and who she wants to be in attendance. You may need to take charge, because she will have her hands full.

3. Be prepared with everything your wife and your newborn will need at the hospital *before* your wife goes into labor. For example, buy a car seat and have you and your wife's delivery bags ready to go (see the end of this section for some ideas on what goes into these bags). Enlist the help of your mother or mother-in-law on this task. She will know what to do and bring. Don't ask your father. Things have changed substantially since you were born. Dads are actually encouraged to be in the room with their wives nowadays.

4. Pray. Or meditate. A lot. You will need divine intervention to help you find peace as you witness your beloved wife in the most extreme pain of her life. This can be traumatizing for some. Remember, millions of other valiant mothers have already participated in this blessed event.

So, brothers, learn from someone who has been through six birthing experiences (including my own) and be grateful for a strong companion who is willing to bear children so that you can be a father, because from my perspective no calling in the world is better than "father."

From Her Perspective

Mom: Hey, Lacey, I used your toothbrush last night.

Lacey: *What?!* That's gross, Mom! I can't believe you used *my* toothbrush!

Ruth (Lacey's sister): Well, you used *her* stomach!"

Yes, mothers who go through nine difficult months of carrying and then delivering a baby know what it feels like to have their stomachs—and bodies for that matter—used and abused.

Soni is so much tougher than I could ever be. After delivering our first with the help of modern-day medicines, she decided she didn't like feeling separated from her body and the birthing process, so she chose to deliver the remaining four children naturally, without an epidural. Do I think she's crazy? Absolutely. Do I understand? Of course not. So I decided to ask my dear wife about the birthing experience from her very experienced perspective. This is basically how the conversation went:

Soni: It's different for every woman. You can't capture what it's like from just one woman's perspective.

Me: Okay . . . but what was it like for you?

Soni: It was painful . . . and amazing.

Me: And?

Soni: Well, it's really amazing how your entire body focuses all its energy on doing one thing, birthing the baby. You know you will experience extreme pain at least every two minutes when you go natural [without meds]. It's like clockwork. Your body knows what to do; it's on autopilot, and there is nothing you can do to stop it. So it's painful and amazing all at once.

Me: Doesn't sound very amazing to me. All that pain?

Soni: It's too hard to describe in words. I mean, it is like nothing else I have ever experienced. You experience such extreme pain one moment and then such extreme joy the next. You could never understand.

Me: So it's kind of like being married to me? Extreme pain and joy?

Soni: No. Not even close . . . well, maybe the pain part . . .

MOM'S DELIVERY BAG (ACCORDING TO SONI)

In general, hospitals will provide most of what a mother needs, but after giving birth to five babies, Soni thought she would provide some suggestions for a mom's delivery bag.

- A good book. You are actually going to have time to yourself, so enjoy it. (It's sad that my wife actually likes going to the hospital because she feels like that is the only time she has to herself. Boy do I have some things to change at home.)

- Comfortable pajamas. They provide you with the hospital gown with all its uncomfortable flaps and abundant airflow, but you may want the comfort of your own jammies.

- Comfortable change of clothes for traveling home (could be the jammies if you like).

- A couple of pairs of underwear. They also give you cool diapers to wear for leakage and stuff. Soni was happy to give hers up in favor of her own underwear, though.

- Nursing pads and creams. Luckily, nursing tips and tricks typically start at the hospital with the help of knowledgeable nurses. But not all creams or pads are created equal. If this is your first time, ask someone who has been through this experience for her opinion and suggestions.

- Nursing bras. These make nursing a whole lot easier.

- Comfortable traveling outfit and blankets for the baby.

DAD'S DELIVERY BAG (ACCORDING TO ME)

Hey, we have feelings too.

- iPad/tablet loaded with favorite movies (Soni and I watched *Nacho Libre* just before she went into the homestretch with one of our children).

- Pair of clean underwear for you. Hey, you never know.

- Camera (phone with camera *if* it's a good camera).

- Toothbrush and toothpaste. In case you lose your lunch.

- Favorite treats.

- Car seat. If you don't bring this, you cannot leave the hospital with your new baby.

PARENTAL AGORAPHOBIA

Agoraphobia is the fear of being in a public situation that will create embarrassment or bring on a panic attack, or of finding yourself in uncontrollable social situations.[1]

If you are a parent, you are probably saying, "Hey, this definition looks and feels very familiar." Think about it. Taking your crew into the great unknown inevitably leads to uncontrollable situations, panic attacks, and fear of what may happen. In other words, most parents suffer from agoraphobia, and the following real-life story explains why.

"One day I found myself at Claire's with my three kids. It was an abnormally busy store with three policeman and one mall security man reprimanding a fourteen-year-old girl for shoplifting; a middle-aged lady with her whole family, waiting to get her ears pierced; two employees—one talking to the police, leaving only one to help the customers; and at least three other moms with their kids. And my loud son, James, who wanted to play with the sunglasses and the necklaces, and everything else in that miserable store.

"Somehow, James, age two, who was strapped into his stroller, managed to squirm his way out of the top of his straps, and in the process, his shorts and his Pull-Up. Unfortunately, I didn't notice any of this until he stood up in the stroller and it was crashing to the ground. The Bath and Body Works bag hanging from the handle ripped in half, and out toppled hand soap, wallflowers, and lotion. Then my attention turned to my son—the one who was naked in the middle of Claire's. That's when I felt my face go red."

Sound familiar? How about this next story? One Sunday in church, I overheard a discussion between a mother and her noisy little boy on the bench in front of me. It went something like this:

"Nick, you need to be reverent in church."
"Why?"
"Because Jesus is here, and he wants us all to be reverent."
(Nick, at the top of his lungs) "JESUS ISN'T HERE! I CAN'T SEE HIM. WHERE'D HE GO?"

Luckily, most of us parents eventually develop the ability to block out the socially unacceptable behavior of our offspring and save ourselves from the associated stress. Some call this selective hearing. I call it survival.

THE SHINY OBJECT TRICK

Distraction works. Especially for babies and toddlers, but teenagers have also been known to fall for, "Hey, did you hear about what Miley Cyrus did last night?" (a reference to the 2013 Video Music Awards debacle). And in this specific example, you have an opportunity to get your children's take on appropriate and inappropriate behavior and to reinforce correct principles as needed.

Changing the subject will sometimes do the trick if the topic you are introducing is something that your children are interested in—or at least fascinated by. With our younger children, we have a lot of "shiny objects" to throw at them to change the subject or distract them. Some of my trademark, go-to tricks to get my toddlers to eat their food include dancing like a geeky father (not hard to do) and singing catchy eighties songs.

However, the key to success with the shiny object trick is the *other* parent. While I am putting on a performance worthy of an Oscar, my incognito wife is sneaking small bites of veggies into the laughing and smiling mouths of our children. Mission accomplished.

This no longer works for our older children, who think their dad is a nerd and have uncovered the undercover parent technique. With them you have to sincerely engage them in relevant discussion. Here are some discussion starters that may work as a distraction technique (personalize as needed):

- Who knows when [name of fun kid movie] will be in the theaters?

- So where do you want to go on vacation this year?

- Where should we go for dessert tonight?

- How do you like [name of book your child is reading]?
- And my favorite—Have I told you about the time I almost died? (Everyone has a near-death experience. If you don't, make one up. Well, maybe not, but you can tell them about how someone you knew almost died.)

Caution! If you're not creative enough or don't change up your approaches often, your kids will figure out your trick and respond back in smart-aleck ways, like Mark did in this story:

> "Mark, your goal right now is to stop playing Xbox and be the first person in the car with their seatbelt on.
>
> "No, that's not my goal. My goal is to get good at electronics, and I have to focus on one goal at a time."

For some additional ideas on discussion starters, check out John and Tina Bushman's book, *Table Talk*.

DON'T FORGET THE POTTY!

I don't know if you have ever noticed how actors never (or rarely) go to the restroom in the movies or in TV shows. Maybe it's because it's too mundane unless it's overly exaggerated and gross like the bathroom scene in *Dumb and Dumber*.

Or maybe there is no entertainment value or purpose to portraying such an everyday behavior. Either way, I believe we, like the writers and directors of movies, also forget that our children need to perform this natural act quite a few times during the day. So we leave our homes, cram into our Suburbans, and reach our destination usually to discover that someone needs to go potty. When mother nature calls, it's never at a convenient time. Nope, it's always right in the middle of a movie, while at a restaurant, or while shopping for clothes or groceries. This usually leads to a mad scramble to find a restroom before you have to return home and change clothes. Even if you make it in time, chances are that in thirty minutes another child will need to go, leading to the same mad scramble.

Here are three easy steps to help you survive the potty dilemma:

Step 1. Make *everyone* go to the restroom *before* you leave home to go anywhere. I always forget this most important survival tip and end up wiping down some gross toilet seat in some men's restroom so that my child can go potty—or waiting outside the women's restroom for my older daughters, looking like a weirdo. I haven't found too many public restrooms I can classify as being as clean or safe as home. So if I can skip this uncomfortable-for-everyone practice, I will, and so should you. I would recommend delegating the responsibility of reminding everyone to go to the restroom before leaving to one of your older children. That way there are at least two of you thinking about this step. This step is so important that you could even put up a banner, poster, or sticky note on the door you usually leave from to remind you.

Step 2. Know the location of every coffee shop or store with a public restroom within fifteen miles of your house because, chances are, one of the kids did not follow step 1. The chain coffee shops give out stickers, which make a nice reward if the child performs as expected.

Step 3. Keep a potty pack in your car. This is different from a diaper bag because it may not contain diapers at all. Even if your kids are no longer in diapers, you never know when you may need an extra pair of undies, wipes, toilet paper, and plastic bags to put the soiled packages in. The older your kids get, the less likely it is they will use this pack, but if you have toddlers and younger kids, it is a great idea. Being prepared is better than the stinky alternative.

POTTY CHECK

1. How will you remember to have everyone in your family go to the restroom before leaving the house?

2. Do you know where all the restrooms are at all the places you frequent and within a fifteen-mile radius of your home?

3. Do you have a potty pack in your car?

PARENTING CAN BE A BLOODY MESS

I hate to be the one to state the obvious, but blood, wounds, and sickness are an integral part of parenting. It all starts with the messy surprises of childbirth and then becomes part of your daily routine in the form of bumps, bruises, sprains, scratches, colds, and the flu. Both Mom Rule and Dad Rule #3, "Throw-up and Toxic Diapers Come with the Job," remind us that these messy tasks come with the title of parent as well. This is real life.

It also seems that some children are more injury-prone than others. For us it's our middle child, Ruby. She also happens to be our most daring child, which probably explains the real reason for her increased rate of painful encounters. The first time I knew we were in trouble was when she was four. We were cliff jumping at

Lake Powell, and I had just jumped off a twenty-two-foot cliff into the lake when I heard my wife screaming (never a good sign) and saw her pointing to the top of the cliff I had just leapt from. There stood Ruby, in her life jacket, preparing to follow her daddy into the water. Without giving it a second thought, the little daredevil jumped. She was fine—and even went over a few more times. But since then, the poor child has cut her lip open snow tubing, slashed the side of her face falling off her bike, sprained several body parts doing who knows what—not to mention several other incidents involving severe bruising or stitches.

Other children can be even more high maintenance, and they may even show hypochondriac behaviors, like the boy who told his mother, "Mom, I'm either having a stomachache or a heart attack. I don't know which one yet," or, "Mom, I need a Band-Aid. Or maybe a cast."

While you can't anticipate every accident or mishap that could occur, you can be better prepared. Here are a few basic tips to help you deal with real and perceived injuries.

1. **Load up on bandages.** They'll be your biggest friend. The first essential item in anyone's first-aid kit should be Band-Aids. Always stock up on more Band-Aids than you think you'll need because you *will* use them all. Fortunately, most of the blood you'll encounter can be covered up with some disinfectant ointment and a Band-Aid. Band-Aids even help soothe perceived injuries that have no blood or visible abrasion. For example, our youngest will often come to us with an "owie" that can only be cured by placing a Band-Aid on the afflicted area—a remedy we know works for toddlers worldwide.

2. **The most important tool in your first-aid kit is a good thermometer.** There are some amazing thermometers nowadays that are easy to use on crying babies or squirming toddlers. One of the best is a temporal or forehead thermometer that is not invasive to a sick child at all. Parents need this tool in their kit for peace of mind and to know when a doctor or hospital visit is required.

3. **Search the web or apps for answers.** These are other valuable tools that parents can turn to that are not actually found in a physical first-aid kit but rather on a smartphone or computer. All parents should take advantage of the amazing information available on websites like WebMD.com. Many of these sites are regulated and populated by real physicians and specialists. It's a great place to ask questions and understand what your child may be suffering from.

4. **Do *not* prescribe; you are not a doctor.** When it comes to medicines and illnesses, here is a word of caution: try to stay away from prescribing drugs and self-medicating unless you are a doctor. Stick to working on symptoms that manifest themselves on the outside, like bloody noses and cuts. While it is also beneficial to understand some basic symptoms like fevers and rashes, always refer to professionals like your family doctor.

5. **Take a first-aid class.** If you really want to be prepared, take a basic first-aid class or two. You never know when it will come in handy. This is especially true with regards to CPR.

6. **Teach your children what to do in emergencies when you are not around.** Ideally, you would like to be with your kids when danger strikes, but unfortunately this is not something you have control over. What you can control is what you teach your children to do in those situations. The key to this tip is to keep your instructions simple. No more than three steps. Answer some of the following questions to get started: What is the first thing you do in case of [fill in emergency]? Where do you go in case of [fill in emergency]?

THE TEMPORARY ORPHAN PARENTING TECHNIQUE

Have you noticed how children who throw tantrums, yell, cry, and generally embarrass their parents temporarily become orphans? In other words, no one wants to own them or say, "Yes, that loud, obnoxious, screaming child is mine." We tend to try to ignore the offending child and act like we don't know him or her.

We typically try the temporary orphan parenting technique as a last resort, after we have patiently encouraged, bribed, threatened, given "the look," and physically intervened. Maybe we default to this technique because by that stage we are **SRSLY** (seriously) considering giving that child up for adoption, or maybe we just don't know what else to do.

The reality is that sometimes there may not be anything we can do right then and there. It's at these times that we refer to Mom Rule #9, which is "When everything else fails, turn to the basic needs." Your children will have emotional breakdowns, throw tantrums, be extremely grumpy, and literally bounce off the walls. Before you turn to medication, first turn to the basics—sleep, food, exercise, and relaxation. Like adults, kids function better if they sleep well, eat healthy, exercise enough, and are not overly stressed.

Chances are, your child is just tired or hungry, and once that basic need has been met, he or she will be back to normal. But you can try a few parenting tricks to reduce the severity and stress of the situation. For starters, have your child's favorite snacks, blankie, bottle, or toy with you at all times—things that can potentially calm him or her down. This may require that you buy a large backpack to accommodate all of these specialty items, but if you have ever experienced one of those impossible moments, you'll agree that it's probably worth it.

REALITY CHECK

WHAT'S IN YOUR BAGGIE?

What snacks, toys, and other items can you start carrying around with you to help calm your child in those difficult times?

ENDNOTE

1.   Wikipedia, s.v. "Agoraphobia," last modified January 17, 2004, http://en.wikipedia.org/wiki/Agoraphobia.

3. THE REALITY YEARS BETWEEN TODDLERS & TEENS

COWS AND KIDS

My neighbor is a father of ten children and grandfather to forty-three grandchildren, so when he talks about raising kids, I listen. He also grew up on a farm and often uses good ol' farmer logic when sharing his wisdom.

One of the many parenting lessons I have received from this wise man came as we stood in my vegetable garden leaning on shovels. He started by saying, "Kids are like cows." I thought to myself, *Of course they are . . . uh . . . what do you mean?*

As he continued to talk, I started to see the similarities between cows and kids (the human kind, not the goat kind).

"Cows are usually penned up in a pasture for the winter, especially in cold climates like where we live. When the spring comes and you open up their pens, the young stock will run and run and run until they cannot run anymore, which is why it's important to put up a fence surrounding their enclosure, or else you will be spending a lot of time trying to track down all of your young runaway cows." Then he transformed into Yoda before my eyes and said, "But Treion, this is the key: you must make sure they have enough feed in the pasture, or else they'll think the grass is greener on the other side."

This is where the parenting analogy comes in.

1. First of all, don't "pen up," or control, your children so much that they will run away as soon as they can. This is also known as being a "helicopter parent"—a phrase first coined in the 1969 bestselling book *Between Parent & Teenager* by Dr. Haim Ginott[1]—which refers to parents who hover like a helicopter over their children.

2. Give them enough room to run. Allow them room to grow.

3. Provide boundaries. The boundary is like the fence being placed close enough to watch over but not so close that they feel imprisoned. Children need to know their boundaries. These boundaries need to be clear and unmoving, because your children will test them. Consistency in parenting is key. If the fence were to move in and out on a daily basis, your children would be confused and unsure of what is expected of them.

4. Give them enough feed. In other words, provide them with everything they need to grow so that they do not look elsewhere for those basic human needs. Think of Maslow's hierarchy of needs.[2] According to Maslow, everyone has five types of needs—physiological (physical requirements for human survival: sleep, food, and water); safety (emotional and physical); feelings of belonging and love; esteem (all humans need to feel like they are respected); and self-actualization and self-transcendence (living up to one's full potential).

DO YOU TREAT YOUR CHILDREN LIKE COWS?

Take a moment to do some serious introspection about how much you control or try to control your children.

1. In your opinion, are you too controlling and strict with your children? What is your spouse's opinion about your parenting style with regards to control?

2. How about your spouse? How does he or she do with this reality parenting principle?

3. How could you get an honest answer to the first question from your children?

4. What boundaries have you put in place to protect your children from running too far away?

5. Does everyone know what those boundaries are?

6. How consistent are you with enforcing those boundaries?

7. Do your children have enough freedom to grow?

8. Are you providing them enough "feed" (basic human needs)?

MAKING IT UP AS YOU GO
IS PERFECTLY NORMAL

One mom was getting tired of her small kids putting dirt in their dog's food. She asked them repeatedly to stop and even explained that Scout (the dog) didn't like dirt in his food. Neither reason nor punishments stopped the little pranksters who continued to sprinkle dirt into his bowl. That's when she channeled her creative genius. So one evening at dinner, she dished up a small portion of dinner on each if their plates, and then making sure they were all watching, sprinkled dirt on top of their food. They never spoiled Scout's food again!

Most of us "parents in motion" channel our creative juices all the time. Heck, I just made a diaper out of paper towels and duct tape the other day because Junior had a blowout and we had just run out of Huggies. No one taught me how to do that. I just made it up on the fly in the same way that many of you do.

You have very unique challenges and issues to deal with as a parent. Your children are different, their personalities are different, and what goes on in your life is uniquely catered to you. Sometimes there is *not* one rule or piece of advice for the specific situation you find yourself in. When you find yourself in a bind, you use your imagination and creativity. Sometimes that's all that stands between you and your sanity. Like the parents who used the Tooth Fairy to their advantage:

My Dearest Emily,

I came by tonight to retrieve your tooth and leave your payment; however, because of the condition of your bedroom, I had a horrible time getting to your bed safely. Once I was there, I was unable to locate the tooth pillow due to the amount of pillows, blankets, and stuffed animals in your bed.

I will have to come by on a different night. Perhaps you can take the time between now and then to properly clean and organize your room. I bet if you ask your mother NICELY, she will even help you to do it.

Much love,

The Tooth Fairy

While I am not advocating that you lie to your children, I am suggesting that there are times when you should be creative in how you present the truth. How you do this is up to you. If you do not feel comfortable in stretching the truth at all, then don't do it. When your kids ask you if Santa Claus is real, you are welcome to tell them no and that you are Santa. Millions of children over the years have been told this secret and have survived the truth. As with most parenting principles, there is not just one right way.

For example, a more direct approach to disciplining comes from the ingenious parents who invented the "get along shirt" for fighting siblings. The picture that has gone viral shows two unhappy children sharing a large white T-shirt with "get along" written across the front. Another couple we know makes their fighting kids hug each other until they both start laughing. I must admit, when I saw this being enforced I nearly peed my pants laughing because of how unhappy the two culprits looked at being forced to embrace someone they utterly despised at that moment.

My uncle's default punishment when he caught his two boys arguing was to have them put on boxing gloves and duke it out. While this isn't a practice I would recommend, the principle of letting your children work it out is a good one. You'll be pleasantly surprised at how your children can use their imagination to solve problems.

One mother who always tried to have her children work out their problems among themselves shared how her youngest, age five, surprised everyone by suggesting her solution would be to "meditate." She then proceeded to sit down on the floor, cross her legs, close her eyes, and hold her palms outstretched, and then she chanted, "Ohmmmm, my sister is dummmmb." Needless to say, the whole family burst into laughter, and the whole issue was completely forgotten.

These are just a few examples of this reality in practice. Making it up as you go is what most parents have to do to get by. The principle for parents to remember in this chapter is that you are all capable of engaging your imagination and creativity to overcome challenging situations. Often these hidden talents only surface when we are completely frustrated and out of rational ideas. It's then that we must plumb our minds and hearts and unearth some of our best ideas and parenting remedies.

Reality Disclaimer

I realize that not all creative solutions, and especially some cited in this chapter, are the most effective way to parent. But sometimes parents do not have time to stop what they are doing, pull down a parenting manual, read what they should do, and then apply that behavior. While they should find time to read these good books, in reality they will most likely not do so in the heat of battle. It's then that they must try to recall what they have read in the past and then use their imaginations to apply what they think is best in that specific moment with that specific child. If they do not follow all of the rules and protocols with exactness, I think they'll be just fine. And, as you'll see later on in this chapter, failure *is* an option as long as we learn from those failures and do better next time.

YOU LIVE IN A BARN AND A PIGSTY

Once you have children, your home becomes their home too, which means doors will be left open (you live in a barn) and bedrooms will be covered in clothing and junk (you live in a pigsty).

This is a fact of parenting unless you are a member of the small group of very lucky parents who have given birth to "golden" children. You know, the ones who actually make their beds and fold their clothes and generally clean up after themselves. We have one of these golden children in our extended family. Believe it or not, our nephew sleeps on the floor most nights, so his bed is always made. True story. In addition, he also folds and organizes his clothes and socks meticulously in all his drawers. Sure, he probably has some other issues to deal with, but regarding the topic of cleaning, he is golden.

But as for the rest of us parents who birthed typical barn-and-pigsty kids, how do we survive the shock of walking into a son's bedroom and finding a year-old slice of pizza neatly wrapped in pair of very used underwear? Well, after screaming into his filthy pillow, we keep trying to teach him sound principles of cleanliness, and we never give up. Most children will outgrow this stage. Most.

At the moment, my wife and I are struggling to accept this reality, and we continue to fight the fact that our home is a mess most of the time and that our children will leave the door open, especially when we have the air conditioning on high.

Even though Soni is a stay-at-home mom and spends most of her days cleaning up our barn and pigsty, she is consistently amazed at how quickly things revert back to the way it was before she cleaned. If you break down what happens when our five kids all get back from school, you get a sense of how things get messy again.

Within minutes of their noisy arrival back home, you have least ten shoes, five coats, five backpacks, various homework folders, textbooks, lunch bags, pens, pencils, candy wrappers, other miscellaneous pieces of trash, and a whole bunch of random trinkets that magically appear from within pockets and bags. Guess where this pile of stuff all ends up? Yes, on our living room floor. The same area my wife spent the morning cleaning and vacuuming. This trail of destruction then slowly but steadily makes it way down the hallway and into every bathroom and bedroom in the house—like a tornado meticulously leaving behind a trail of destruction in its wake.

We've discussed the phenomenon as a family, assigned specific places in our home where different stuff belongs, and even doled out punishment for contributing to the pigsty. Nothing changed. Same stuff, different day. It's probably time we accept the inevitable—we live in a barn and a pigsty. Maybe you'll have more success by applying the reality parenting principles found in this book—especially the one in the next section.

CHORE CHART CONSISTENCY

I have spoken to dozens of parents about chores and charts and stickers and stars and rewards and Disney celebrations. And I've come to the realization that most chore charts just don't work the way we think they will.

We have tried thirty different iterations ourselves, and it still doesn't make our kids do the work. What gets our kids to do their chores is *not* the chart, no matter how fancy and magical it may look. *What gets our children to do the work is us and our best friend, consistency.*

The very small percentage of parents who swear by their creative pyramid chore chart are also the same parents who are the most consistent at reminding their children to do their chores. Most kids are not self-motivated enough to be inspired by flashy charts in the long run. Yes, in the short term they will be excited about adding gold stars to their Barbie- or Toy Story–themed scoreboard, but that will wane quickly.

However, if a chore chart or scoreboard is what keeps *you*, the parent, on track with *their* chores, then keep on using them. We do. They just look a whole lot worse than they originally did. Actually, we just write their chores on a lined piece of paper every week and hold them accountable for doing them.

As you may have gathered by now, this section is not so much about chore charts, which are just one example. The real parenting principle I wish to emphasize is consistency. After all, it applies to almost every facet of parenting, including how you discipline.

Reality parenting is about consistency, not perfection. In other words, use chore charts (or other forms of scoreboards) even if they don't work.

However, if you do want some fun chore chart ideas for children of all ages, including the teens, refer to *How to Get Kids to Help at Home* by Elva Anson.[3]

The Fun with Chore Charts Game

If you, like us, have resigned to using basic chore charts—such as a list on lined paper—you can use this to your advantage with a game you can play with your kids.

Simply give an award to the child who has used his or her original chart for the longest time. It doesn't matter if it's tattered and torn or dirty and worn. As long as it is still functional and legible (kind of), it qualifies. Frame it and give an award with a cash prize or some other gift.

"THE BIRDS AND THE BEES"
ARE FOR THE BIRDS

As I was contemplating how I was going to start the "birds and the bees" talk with one of my kids, I realized how absurd that term was. Who on earth came up with "the birds and the bees" anyway? And what do birds and bees have to do with sex? I could imagine a conversation with one of my kids going like this (with thoughts in parentheses):

Me: Okay, honey, we are going to talk about the birds and the bees now. (*Crap! How do I make the connection between bees and sex?*) It's important for you to know that what a bee does to a flower is . . . very similar to what your daddy did to your mommy so we could have you.

Child: You did something to mommy? (*What is he talking about now?*)

Me: Well, yes . . . you know a bee carries pollen to flowers so that they can pollinate or grow, right?

Child: Yes. (*Okay . . . sounds like what my teacher was talking about.*)

Me: Well, I carried a certain . . . type of pollen into your mommy's . . . flower so that she could . . . grow with you. Does that make sense? (*I sure hope so, because that was hard to explain. I don't want to try explaining it using birds . . . Come to think of it, I don't even think I know how birds "do it."*)

Child: Yes . . . (*No, not really, but this talk has gotten really weird. What flower does my mommy have, and why does dad think he is a bee? My dad is really weird.*)

Me: Great. If you ever have any more questions about sex, please let me know. (*Or talk to your mother.*)

Child: Okay . . . (*SEX! That's what he has been talking about!*)

BTW (by the way), I dug a little deeper and discovered that this traditional, culturally imbedded phrase, *the birds and bees*, was started to "explain the mechanics and good consequences of sexual intercourse."[4]

Wow! When you really think about it, bees carrying pollen and depositing it into flowers is really an abstract metaphor, and I really don't want to be confusing my kids. Sure, I want them to understand the basic mechanics and definitely the consequences, but in human terms (and, of course, in the PG version). With this in mind, you should keep four things in mind about having "the talk":

1. Have "the talk" as early as possible

If you don't have "the talk" face-to-face, count on technology, TV, magazines, and friends teaching their "quickie" and perverse versions to your children. Just turn on the television and you'll see sex sold in thirty-second commercials, made reference to in every prime-time show, and acted out with innuendo and even sexually explicit footage. Even the magazine racks at your neighborhood grocery store boldly advertise topics on their covers like "10 Ways to Please Your Man" or "What Every Man Should Do in Bed." Our children are not blind or stupid. They see what we do, read what we read, and hear what we talk about. It's essential to talk frankly about sex and to do so early on. For some great advice on what age you should start talking to your child about sex, check out healthychildren.org under the Ages & Stages tab.[5] And when you have "the talk", please don't ever refer to birds or bees. It's *sex* or *sexual relations*, not *pollination*.

2. Use anatomically correct terminology.

It is important to teach your kids the correct anatomical names of body parts, because if you or your wife were not around when one of our children got hurt, they could share with the doctors the name of the correct body part that was hurt. Using slang terms for body parts could lengthen the time for diagnosis as medical staff try to piece together what your kids are talking about. Here is a wonderful illustration of how one mother was able to discover how little her two daughters understood:

The mom started the conversation with, "The area below your belly button will undergo some pretty big changes during puberty. And there is no turning back. Do you know what a vagina is?" Neither one of them did.

Mom: "It's the hole that you push a baby out of."

Daughter 1: "I thought babies came out of your foot."

Mom: "What?"

Daughter 2: Yes, you know when a lady lies down on an exam table and the doctor is sitting near her feet, and then she pushes the baby out."

Sounds like TV had given these two a distorted idea of what childbirth is like. Luckily, it was an innocent version. Another boy came up to his dad and said, "Dad, do you want to see my ding dong?" A little surprised, his father said, "Um, okay?" The boy then lifted up his shirt and poked his belly button and proudly exclaimed, "Ding Dong!" Needless to say, dad was a bit relieved and realized he needed to teach his son how to use correct terminology.

I must admit that this is hard for me to do, because hearing my young son talk about his "pee-pee" is so cute and innocent.

Luckily, doctors know what "pee-pee" or "willy" means. Right? At least I hope so, because I don't know if I'm ready for him to say "penis" just yet.

3. Have "the talk" in a safe and private location.

One couple told me about their disastrous experience trying to have this talk over breakfast at IHOP (International House of Pancakes). Imagine how embarrassing it was for the child and parents to be talking about such a sensitive topic surrounded by heaps of pancakes, jars of syrup, and nosey servers and strangers. Talk about making an awkward conversation even more awkward.

No, serious conversations deserve a private setting, where all involved feel safe and comfortable to express their questions and concerns. One parent shared how she had this talk while sitting side-by-side on their porch swing. She suggested that it went over much better than when she tried having "the talk" F2F (face to face). Not making eye contact helped decrease the level of discomfort for her daughter.

4. Make sure they understand everything.

And there is a lot to cover. Be patient, be specific, and be prepared for some interesting conversations, like this one:

Child: "What's a virgin?"

Dad: "Ummmm. Someone who hasn't ever had sex."

Child: "Doesn't it also mean a place where grapes grow?"

Dad: "No, that's a *vineyard*."

Child: "Oh . . . I get those two mixed up."

Or the young daughter who discovered condom machines in a bathroom while traveling in Africa and wanted to know about them. After the mother went through the different kinds and discussed their purpose, the daughter was appalled.

"Wait. *Why* would you have sex if you didn't want to have a baby?"

"Because it's a sign of affection."

"So is it a show of affection to have sex with somebody?"

"Yes. It's like kissing."

"I don't get it. I mean. . . why would you need to do that? And why are there condoms in a women's bathroom?"

"Because you can buy them anywhere."

"Every store?"

"Most of them."

"I bet that's really weird for the cashier. I do not *ever* want to be a cashier."

Take time to prepare with your spouse on what to say and how to say it (there are a lot of great books and websites on exactly how to do this), put on your game face, and have "the talk."

PARENTAL WARNING

Keep your door open for questions but closed for practice. While it is essential for your children to come to you to talk about anything, especially sex, you always want to ensure you lock your doors when practicing. You do not want your children to walk in on you and your spouse and see something that could haunt them forever.

My friend Alex shared a discussion he had with his eleven-year-old boy around his upcoming wedding anniversary:

"What are you and Mom doing to celebrate your wedding anniversary?"

"We will probably go out to dinner and a movie."

"Well, I want you to have some fun. It's a special occasion, so you and Mom should have sex."

"Umm, okay . . . so what do you mean by 'we should have sex'?"

"Well you know, like when you guys lie on the bed and kiss and hold each other."

"Oh, right!"

That short story teaches us three things. One, Alex's son feels comfortable enough to talk to his dad about sex. Two, Alex should lock the door. Three, it's time for Alex and his son to have "the talk."

REALITY CHECK

"THE TALK"

1. Have you had "the talk" with all your kids? If not, when will you? How will you start? What are some conversation starters?

2. What terms do you children use to refer to their reproductive organs that they probably shouldn't use anymore?

THE WEDGIE POLICE

One reality of parenting is that your children will tell you all about your imperfections and character flaws. If you want an unbiased opinion on anything, ask your children, but,beware: they can be brutally honest.

According to my children, I apparently have a severe case of the wedgies. They have dutifully informed me that I "always" have a wedgie, which is a cause of much laughter and ridicule in my home. Instead of being offended by this potentially embarrassing revelation, I have chosen to embrace my "flaw" and, with the help of my Wedgie Police, even created a special signal for those times I am an offender. So whenever my pants seek refuge where they should not, my children will clap in a very unique way to alert me. Whenever that happens, which does seem to be rather often, I perform a crazy gyration and silly dance to undo the mess. I know, probably **TMI** (too much information), but there you have it: the author suffers from chronic "wedgie-itis."

Here are a few different ways you can react to your kids' criticism:

1. You can *ignore* the criticism, but that will not guarantee that it will stop.

2. You can *get mad,* but that just makes things uncomfortable, and they will just mock you behind your back.

3. You can *cry*, which will probably make them stop, but also make them feel really bad. This should not be your intent.

4. You can *laugh* along with them, which is probably the best choice.

Remember one of the first realities in the book, "You are not perfect"? Well, think of your children as helping you remember this reality, and remember that perfection shouldn't be your goal anyway. So, if you have a perceived flaw, then so be it. Take it all in stride . . . and in my case, with a little wiggle as I waddle to ensure I don't have a wedgie.

Funny side note: I shared the Wedgie Police story with my Facebook friends and one replied, "**LOL** [laughing out loud]. Great kids. *They've really got your back*." Very funny, Yvonne . . . very funny.

REALITY CHECK

WHAT'S MY WEDGIE?

1. What do your kids tease you about? Is it your clothes? The music you listen to? Your haircut? Lack of hair? The way you walk? The way you talk (Groovy)? Or something else?

2. How will you choose to react when teased? What is your game plan?

SIX DEGREES OF "DUMB"

Your kids are going to do dumb things. I know, this is an obvious reality, but if it's so obvious, then why do we get all upset when they do dumb things? Maybe we think our kids are exempt or that they couldn't possibly do what other kids do. Whatever the reason, be prepared for dumb, because that is also a parenting reality.

My definition of "dumb" is participating in behaviors, due

to peer pressure, curiosity, or reckless abandonment, with the knowledge that said behavior can be detrimental to the physical, emotional, and social health and well-being of oneself or others.

Some "dumb" behaviors are natural and should not be blown out of proportion, while other behaviors are more severe and can be harmful to our children and other people. Here are six Degrees of Dumb you may be able to relate to:

First Degree—Spilling the milk. "Mom, I tripped and spilled my drink all over your new couch." (Root idiom—*It's no use crying over spilled milk*, which means it's no use being upset about making the mistake because you cannot change that now.)

This first degree of dumb is actually something that is rather common with most human beings, not just children. We all trip, spill stuff, drop things, and make a mess. Children's motor skills and coordination are just not as dialed in as us older folk. However, some people and kids just have a greater propensity to spill things than others. We call them "clumsy" or "accident-prone." It's really not an indication of intelligence. They are not dumb; they're just more accident prone than most.

In this case, I disagree with the advice given to Forrest Gump by his mother, "Stupid is as stupid does."[6] Sometimes all of us do what may be perceived as stupid things because of pure unluckiness, accident, or just plain ignorance, which doesn't make us stupid. Like the daughter who asked her mother, "Mom, there was this day a week or two ago that I dropped some mail off the porch into the bushes. Did you get it?"

Second Degree—Spilling the beans. "My dad has a super hairy back." (Root idiom—*Spill the beans*, which means to give away a secret or surprise.)

The unfortunate reality is that your children will share family secrets, private experiences, how much money you make, and a plethora of other potentially personal and embarrassing info with their friends and their parents. We have had to tell our kids a few times that what happens at home stays at home (a G-rated version of the Las Vegas advertising campaign "What Happens in Vegas Stays in Vegas.")

This behavior is not limited to talkative toddlers but also to troublesome teens. If you are not careful, you will have neighbors and strangers alike knowing far too much about you, your body, and your business. In my case, my chronic problem with wedgies (see the previous section on The Wedgie Police) has found its way into the "surbubosphere," which is partly why I am now okay with sharing it with the world in this book.

Third Degree—Testing the waters. "I wonder how hot that is? I should touch it and see." (Root idiom—*Test the waters*, which means to try something new)

Testing boundaries, like touching a hot oven top with your hand to see if it is hot, jumping off the roof, and biting into a jalapeño comes with the territory. Fortunately, this level of curiousness is usually a one-time experience, and siblings who witness the negative side effects of their unlucky brother or sister usually do not try the same test.

Some things are worthy of testing; others are not. You may want to share the consequences of those things that are not worthy of testing with your kids before they try it themselves. Even with parental warnings, kids will still jump off rooftops into your bushes and break their ankles (I'm talking about you, Isaac). But at least you know you tried to warn them. In my opinion, the ability to reason seems to be dramatically reduced during the teenage years.

Fourth Degree—Playing with fire. "We got bored so we made this awesome fire bomb . . ." (Root idiom—*Play with fire*, which means if you do something dangerous, you will get hurt.)

The feeling of invincibility also comes with adolescence, which often result in dangerous risks and stupid behaviors like driving too fast with a car full of your friends or mixing dangerous chemicals to see what happens. Unfortunately, the consequences associated with this Degree of Dumb are much more serious than the previous one and can even be fatal. Let's hope your children don't make it past the third degree to this or subsequent Degrees of Dumb. But if they do, you need not only to speak up but also in many cases intervene (see the "Say What You Need to Say" section).

Some dumb things should not be tolerated. I have personally witnessed how difficult intervention can be as loving parents confront and work with a troubled teen. It strains them emotionally and financially. It is hard, but when you love a child that much, you will sacrifice whatever it takes to protect him or her from additional bad decisions. While this reality may sometimes feel like it requires a pound of flesh, remember not to allow one child's decisions to adversely affect your relationship with your other children or your spouse. Each situation is different, so only you will know where to draw the line and when to move on.

Fifth Degree—Flying in the face of danger. "But, Dad, everyone is doing it!" (Root idiom—*Fly in the face of danger*, which means to take great risks or to threaten or challenge danger.)

"Everyone is doing it" works well for a new flavor of ice cream or a new roller coaster ride without resulting in negative long-term consequences (unless your child continues to eat too much of the ice cream, of course). However, there are many things that your children should never try, even once: all addictive substances such as drugs, smoking, alcohol, and the like. Peer pressure and trying something to fit in are the major influencing factors and causes of this kind of stupidity among teens.

I grew up with an alcoholic mother who also smoked like a chimney. I remember getting a bottle of sherry for my twelfth birthday and trying a cigarette that same year. Even though I haven't drunk sherry for over twenty-six years, I still remember how it tastes and will sometimes salivate thinking about it. My brother picked up my mother's smoking habit and now smokes all the time. Children shouldn't ever be introduced to addictive substances, but a survey by Columbia University's CASA reveals that "86 percent of American high school students say that some classmates are drugging, drinking, and smoking during the school day, and almost half know a student who sells drugs at their school."[7]

Whether you want to believe it or not, your children have access to substances that can change their lives forever. What are you going to do about it? (Take a look at "The Teenager Agreement" section for some ideas.)

Sixth Degree—Breaking the law. "I don't know what I was thinking." (Root idiom—*To break the law*, which means to fail to obey a law or to act contrary to a law.)

This is the pinnacle of the Degrees of Dumb Pyramid and the level that has the severest penalties. Breaking the law in all its variances has automatic consequences already built in. There are no "get out of jail free" cards in the game of life. You've probably heard the phrase "Don't do the crime if you can't do the time," but have you really thought of about it? Have you spoken to your children in plain and explicit terms about crime?

I have a good friend whose son was just convicted of manslaughter and will now spend at least the next fifteen years of his young and promising life in prison. While he made a lot of dumb decisions leading up to that one action, choosing to kill another man was his choice, and sadly he will now have to face the consequences.

The reality parenting principle in this section is to do whatever you can to make sure your children stay away from degrees three through six. Your responsibility as a parent is to be the Dumb Tsar. You decide what Degree of Dumb is acceptable, and then talk frankly and openly with your kids about what is and is not acceptable and what the consequences for being dumb are. Don't be dumb yourself and believe that your children will learn what it means to be a responsible and upstanding human being and citizen all by themselves. That is your job. If not you, then who?

REALITY CHECK

WHAT DEGREE OF DUMB ARE MY KIDS?

1. Take some time alone or with your spouse to evaluate where your children are on the Degrees of Dumb Pyramid.

2. Use the following discussion starters to have the "dumb" talk with your kids if necessary:

- "It is safe (appropriate) in our home for you to [insert relevant behaviors]?"

- "It is not safe (or appropriate) for you, your friends, or any of us to [insert relevant behaviors]."

- "It is important for you to understand the consequences for doing [insert dumb behavior], so let's [watch a YouTube video or talk to someone who has paid the price—or just talk about the realities together].

- And in some cases "Your mother (or father) and I are concerned that your [insert relevant behavior] will cause you harm. Can we share our feelings about this with you?"

In severe cases, you will need to decide on what actions and interventions you, as a parent, need to make in order to protect your child—no matter what it takes.

LEFTOVERS AND AFRICA

"Stop being so picky and eat your food. Do you know how many starving children in Africa would love to eat what you have in front of you?"

This statement, or some variation of it, is probably one all parents have made at one time or another. *Fortunately*, most of our children may never truly understand what it means to go hungry. *Unfortunately*, because most children don't know what real hunger feels like, they may believe they can be picky about what they eat. I like how one boy let his mother know he didn't like what she had cooked: "Mom, I think you *accidentally* used the wrong ingredients." At least he's creative.

I grew up in Africa, and I know what it means to go hungry. We lived on the outskirts of the large concrete jungle, Johannesburg, in the poor district. My single mother worked hard to provide for her two sons, but sometimes we just went without or ate whatever we had. I remember frying up squash for a dinner because it was easy to come by or making "leftover stew" with whatever was in the house. Peanut butter sandwiches were also a staple in our flat and a snack I still enjoy today. While my impoverished state was bad at times, it was not even close to the real poverty and starvation that so many children live with and die from in third-world countries. However, when I hear my children complain about the vegetables or eggs or whatever on their plates, I have to constrain myself and remember that they have not experienced what I have experienced and do not know what I know.

While there are many parenting angles to this reality, I am going to focus this section on the principles of excess and waste. In our culture, we typically have more than enough food and other material possessions, which leads to excessive waste. Just look at how much food you throw away after each meal. A Tristram Stuart report suggests that there are nearly one billion malnourished people in the world, but the approximately forty million tons of food wasted by US households, retailers, and food services each year would be enough to satisfy the hunger of every one of them.[8]

While theoretically this is true, it's obviously not easy to practice. Once we have dished a meal onto a plate, it becomes a perishable item and not fit to ship to your neighborhood soup kitchen, not to mention China or Africa. Plus, the FDA (Food and Drug Administration) has stringent laws on what you can and cannot do with leftovers and perishables. Just ask the fast food chains that are mostly to blame for the forty tons of food wasted each year.

However, there are precautions you can take as a family to reduce waste and credible organizations you can donate to. In this way, you and your family can in essence "feed Africa" or any other country for that matter. So what can you do to minimize waste?

Your Family Can . . .

When eating at home:

1. Plan your meals better. Actually write them down, then only buy what's on the list. Simple but efficient.

2. Be creative with food. If you only have a piece of this and a pinch of that, they may go together well in meal you hadn't thought of before. I grew up making stews from the odds and ends my brother and I would find in the kitchen. Fruits getting a little ripe? Make a smoothie or

freeze them to use later. If you have leftovers, then make that your next meal or a part of the next meal. Involve your children in the creativity process. You'll be amazed at the ideas they come up with, and the process teaches them to use what you have. It may not always taste great, but that's a risk you take.

3. Serve smaller portions. If your children want more, you can always dish up more once they have finished what's on their plates.

When going out:

1. Eat before taking your crew out—especially to the movies. If you don't, you'll need a second mortgage to pay for the handful of snacks you buy there. I always feel like I have been mugged when I hand over a ten-dollar bill and get one box of popcorn. Our kids have learned that they have a better chance of being sent to the moon than getting treats at the movie theater. Also, sometimes we'll eat dinner at a restaurant and then make dessert at home.

2. Be clear on what can and cannot be ordered at a restaurant before you sit down. The fifty-dollar twelve-ounce rib eye steak or lobster tail is not an option for any member of our family unless it is a really important occasion. Sharing this rule with your children beforehand is so much better than having the argument with them at the restaurant in front of a dozen strangers.

3. Bring home the leftovers and eat them the next day.

HOW CAN YOU REDUCE WASTE?

1. What can you do to minimize waste at home?

2. How can you and your family contribute to a worth-while charity?

OOPS, I FORGOT!

One reality that we as parents must come to terms with is that our children will suffer from two ailments: selective listening and selective memory. You will spend your entire life asking your children to remember to . . .

"Brush your teeth."

"Practice the piano."

"Take a bath."

"Eat your broccoli."

"Say 'thank you'."

"Finish your homework before you play video games."

"Hand in your assignment."

"Brush your hair before school."

"Make your bed."

"Clean your room."

"Finish your chores, and then you can play with your friends."

"Wear clean underwear."

. . . but there is a good chance you'll end up hearing, "Oops. I forgot you told me to do that."

Sometimes reminding them several times works, but sometimes it doesn't. One communication technique that seems to help is to ask your children to restate back to you what they are expected to do. If what you want them to do is super important, you could also have them write it down and put it up somewhere where they can see it often, like on the refrigerator or the bathroom or vanity mirror. You know they will be frequenting all three of these locations in your home, so why not put that prime real estate to good use?

REALITY CHECK

WHAT DO YOUR CHILDREN TYPICALLY FORGET?

1. Think of the one or two or three things your children usually forget and write them down. You will see a common pattern here. With my children, the two things they selectively choose to ignore are brushing their teeth and cleaning up after themselves in the kitchen.

2. What will you do differently to help them hear better and start acting differently?

SLIPPERY WHEN WET

Annie and her husband were caught off-guard when their six-year-old daughter plopped down on her chair for family dinner one night and innocently called her mother a "MotherF$%&er." Fortunately, her tongue slip was an innocent one. She had learned it watching a movie she shouldn't have and was promptly corrected by her concerned parents.

One of the many great parenting lessons we can learn from the Bible is the principle of taming the tongue. Solomon counseled, "He who restrains his lips is wise" (Proverbs 10:19). Another wise teacher, who goes by the name Anonymous, has taught us to "beware of the tongue; it's in a wet place and slips easily."

Words are more powerful than we can ever imagine. Words have always been instrumental in inciting revolutions, mobilizing movements, inspiring armies, and invoking love. Words have the power to empower, enliven, and encourage, but they can also demean, discourage, and cause despair.

As in most parenting realities, there are two sides, or voices, to this challenge. First, things your children say to you. Second, things you say to them.

Things Children Say

First, you need to be aware that a lot of what your children say in moments of frustration and emotional distress does not reflect their true feelings for you. It's just a manifestation of how they are feeling in that moment, which is why "I hate you" can be seen as a compliment and why "I wish you would just leave me alone (let me live my own life)," really just means, "Please give me some room to breathe and time to think." You've heard it said that it's sometimes hard to find the words to say. Well, when you have only had fourteen to seventeen years to learn the complexities of the English language and you are dealing with a whole bunch of new emotions, it's no wonder our children use words and phrases that don't really reflect what they mean. And this just adds to their frustration, **BTW** (by the way).

Things Parents Say

But we don't have the same excuse. We have already passed through our teenage years and have, I hope, learned how to express ourselves more effectively and control our emotions. We have more responsibility with regards to what we say to our children than what they say to us. Which is why what we say and how we say it is more important than we realize.

Gemma, my four-year-old at the time, with a very sad face said: "Daddy, am I still your favorite child?"

Me: "Of course you are. Why?"

Gemma: "Because you told Chloe (my teenager) she was your favorite."

I then realized that my joke with the kids was not a joke to Gemma. She had scratched my head earlier on in the day, and, with a big grin and a wink, I had called her my favorite child in front of her siblings. Later on that same day, Chloe had helped her mother out with something, and I had called her my favorite child, thinking the kids understood that I was joking with them.

It dawned on me that I should be a little more careful about what I say. I shared this experience with my Facebook friends, and one responded with, "I tell each of them that they are my favorites and the other day they discovered my secret." Another friend shared some advice—Use one definitive thing about each kid: "Layla, you are my *favorite* gymnast!" (She is my only gymnast.) Or, "TJ, you are my favorite son." (He's my only son.) That way, they are all truly your favorites in unbiased ways.

A word of caution: make sure you understand exactly what your children are asking you before you open your mouth and say too much, like this one daddy did with his young daughter.

Daughter: "Daddy, what does swearing mean?"

Daddy: "Well, honey, it's when people say bad words."

Daughter: What bad words?

Daddy: "Well . . . words like hell, damn, b#$%, sh*t."

Daughter: "Oh, that's weird. I thought it was when you make a promise."

Oops!

Beware of the Words and Phrases You Use

How often do we think about the terms or phrases or words we use when talking to our children, or even with our spouses? Are we causing unnecessary anxiety and concern in our children? Do we use extremes like the following when reprimanding a child: "You always [insert behavior]" or "You never [insert behavior]"?

Some of the greatest harm we can cause is to demean impressionable minds with destructive words and phrases like "How can you be so stupid that you [insert other demeaning behavior]?" or "I can't believe you did [behavior]."

If you, like me, are guilty of not sufficiently controlling your tongue, you may consider reading the book *30 Days to Taming Your Tongue: What You Say (and Don't Say) Will Improve Your Relationships* by Deborah Smith Pegues. In her book, Pegues lists thirty types of verbal transgressions and recommends that we eliminate one per day for thirty days. Half-truths, argumentative language, gossiping, slander, belittling, self-absorbed or doubting words, rude or cynical talk, and intimidation are just some of the verbal transgressions described.[9]

Things You Should Say

Besides the many things we should not say, there are hundreds of words and phrases parents should generously hand out as much as they possibly can. "I love you," "Well done," and "I am so proud of you," when sincerely spoken, can empower young minds, fortify against insecurities, and fuel dreams.

REALITY CHECK

WATCH YOUR LANGUAGE

1. What words or phrases can you *stop* using today?

2. What words or phrases can you *start* using today?

SAY WHAT YOU NEED TO SAY

While sometimes it is best for us just to listen, there are also times when we must speak up and even take action.

The best metaphor I've heard regarding *when* to speak up or take action is when your child is any danger (perceived or real). That's when our parenting instinct should kick into gear. For example, if your child is sitting on railroad tracks and there is a train coming, you will surely speak up and warn him or her. You will not be afraid to yell for fear of hurting your child's feelings or stifling his or her freedom of choice. And if your child chooses to ignore your warning, you will probably physically remove him or her from the imminent danger yourself. That's what reality parents do. We sometimes have to act in order to protect our children, especially when they are in danger, and sometimes from themselves.

I realize that your children will most likely not be hanging out on railroad tracks, but they could experiment with drugs or drive while under the influence or participate in a dozen other similarly dangerous activities. That's when we must have the courage to speak up. Out of love. Out of concern. Out of respect for their lives and souls.

They may hate us for our words and actions, and some may fight us and still end up on the tracks. Too many of our youth become addicted to harmful substances and destructive behaviors. We cannot control what choices *they* make, but we can choose how *we* act. We must be courageous in the hard moments and speak up in order to protect our children. It is our duty as parents.

DON'T EAT YOUR CHILDREN; THEY CAN BE TOUGH TO SWALLOW

Children are like kittens. You can overlook the little piddles a kitten has on your couch because he is so cute. But as the kitten grows into a cat, you become less forgiving because the cat is not as cute and they should know by now that they cannot pee on the furniture.

For the past three years, our son, TJ, has woken us up almost every night. While I am always annoyed and frustrated by the little stink, it is hard to get mad when you hear, "Daddy, I want babba, pity peez" (Dad, I want a bottle, pretty please). I tend to overlook him waking us up because of how cute his little face and voice are, but if one of the older kids dares to wake me up, they hear about it.

I realize that patience, regardless of the cuteness level, is needed to be a good parent. Plus, "chewing out" your children is never a good idea. It's often an easy default, and it comes rather naturally when you are frustrated, but that just makes them despise you. Refrain. Control. Patiently, kindly instruct and discipline. This is one reality I have been working on since I became a parent, and, unfortunately, progress is slow.

And no, the "bitter bear face" is not the best approach when it comes to kids either. It makes them afraid of you, and it makes you seem unapproachable. Unless you have a precocious four-year-old, that is. It had been a long week and I was sitting on the couch just staring into space when Gemma asked me, "Daddy, are you mad?"

"No, dear, why do you think I'm mad?"

"Because you have a mean look on your face."

Apparently I had the bitter bear face and didn't know it. My children have told me that I sometimes have "the face," and that it comes across as angry and mean. So now when I find myself stressed out by my kids or just tired, I make a conscious effort not to have it show on my face or in my tone of voice. Even if it means I am forcing a smile. Easier said than done.

THE PLUS OR MINUS TWO FACTOR

When Soni and I were first engaged, we talked for hours about how many kids we would have and how we would raise them in a home filled with fun, love, and learning. We had it all planned out. Fourteen years and five kids later, we are wondering what on earth happened to that plan.

We now spend our days herding kids to do homework and chores and coordinating carpools to and from extracurricular activities. Still, all this we can manage . . . most of the time.

It's when you add in the "Plus or Minus Two Factor" that everything falls apart and chaos reigns. What is the Plus or Minus Two Factor? Simply put, sometimes you have all your kids plus about two friends, and sometimes you are missing about two of your children. (Which for some of you may be all your children.) For example, each of our five kids has a handful of friends who will often drop by the house unannounced, thus adding to the number of kids we have. On other occasions, some of our kids are at their friends' houses or at activities, thus subtracting from the number of kids we have.

Since most *Homo sapiens*, especially the parental kind, like routine and consistency, change can throw things out of whack and spawn unforeseen chaos—the type of chaos that causes you to consider moving away to the countryside where friends are far away and life seems so much simpler. Since running away from the craziness isn't a realistic alternative for us, we have decided as parents to do what we can to fulfill that initial dream by trying to make our home a place where our kids and their friends feel welcome and comfortable no matter how crazy things are.

One thing we try to do is welcome friends to come by before school and have breakfast with us. We find that some of these kids don't have that opportunity at home and like the feeling of sitting down with us before the school day begins. Whatever it is you can do to make your home feel warm and welcoming will not only be good for your kids but for their friends as well. Whether you like it or not, friends come with the job. You might as well try to make the best out of the situation. Otherwise, everyone is going to be miserable, especially you.

So just anticipate that you may have one or two extra kids hanging around for dinner, and you'll reduce the amount of stress . . . at least a little.

Default Behavior—Stock Up on Goodies

It's a fact that kids, especially teenagers, eat a lot. If you don't have the snacks they like, they'll just go somewhere else. We think it is better having our children's friends hanging out at our house, where we know what they are up to, which is why we try to stock up on the foods they like.

There is also a delicate balance between providing too much bad sugar and saturated fat and encouraging healthy eating. I am not saying you should replace your healthy meal strategy and break Mom Rule #25, "Become a Competent Chef," but I am saying you should also stock up on the yummy foods that encourage your kids to stay home instead of wandering the neighborhood.

A son, while looking at the nutrition facts on a box of cereal, told his mom, "Have you seen how much sugar is in these things? You shouldn't let me eat this anymore." And then just two minutes later, "Mom, can I please have some more? Because they taste really good."

Like this real-life interaction shows, I wouldn't be a responsible parent or citizen if I failed to also warn you about the dangers of candy, pop, and chips. According to a new report by the United Nations Food and Agriculture Organization, nearly a third of American (31.8%) adults are defined as obese.[10]

A Better Alternative

In other words, you should also stock up on some healthier alternatives that still taste good and are good for you. My father-in-law has done an amazing job raising his children and influencing mine to drink water instead of soda. He has the whole family calling water "the elixir of life."

While hundreds of fantastic blogs and websites focus specifically on this topic, here are a few of our favorite healthier alternatives:

- Veggies and dip (the secret is getting a tasty dip).

- Watermelon and feta cheese (may sound gross, but the two go very well together).

- Bananas dipped in melted chocolate (chocolate is practically a vegetable).

- Grapes. Frozen grapes also make a tasty treat and good alternative to ice cream (or eat it with ice cream).

- Green smoothies. You can find dozens of recipes online that taste good and are good for you.

- Berry smoothies. Same as above. This works with kids if you position it as making a Jamba or Kiva Juice (or the smoothie franchise in your neighborhood) at home.

- Spinach ice cream. We make our own, and it tastes much better than it sounds.

- Oatmeal cookies. If you're going healthy, then substitute agave instead of sugar and whole wheat for the unhealthy white stuff.

- Cheese sticks. Hey, it's healthy dairy.

- Broccoli and salad dressing (pick a dressing that is sweet, like lemon poppy seed).

- Chips and salsa (especially homemade salsa). There are also healthier chip alternatives.

- Celery and peanut butter—another great combo that doesn't look good on paper but is actually quite yummy.

Just place a few of these treats in front of some hungry teenagers, and they'll not only eat it but enjoy it. Go on, give it a try.

REALITY CHECK

HOW WILL YOU MAKE YOUR HOME "KID APPROVED"?

1. How can you make your home a comfortable and safe place for your children and their friends to hang out?

2. What will your approach to food and snacks be?

3. How can you find out what your children and their friends like to do and eat?

KILLER PEANUTS

For the first few years of her life, Dayna suffered from severe food allergies, which manifested as eczema and asthma. Her skin would get so bad that she would bleed from the creases in her neck and even from her eyelids. At first she couldn't sleep for more than an hour at a time, and her mother and father would take turns gently rubbing and tickling her legs and arms to try to relieve the pain and itching. People would look at Dayna with pity and then stare at her parents with disdain, as if they were abusing the poor child. On one occasion in a grocery store, a woman approached them and shockingly asked, "**OMG** (oh my gosh). What's the matter with your child?" The father, who'd had enough that day, coolly replied, "It's leprosy, but don't worry. It's not contagious." Another time someone asked if she was a burn victim. After extensive testing, doctors determined that Dayna was allergic to peanuts, wheat, eggs, strawberries, avocados, bananas, animal fur/hair, and all kinds of grass. Luckily for Dayna and her exhausted parents, she eventually outgrew most of her allergies and lives a rather normal life today.

This reality is more common than you may be aware of. Almost 10 percent of children today have severe allergies to common foods we all carry in our homes—milk, eggs, soy, peanut butter, wheat, seafood, and fruits.[11] That means at least one in every ten of your children's friends may have severe allergies that you need to be aware of.

Our children have a few friends that cannot even be near the smell of peanuts, which is the most prevalent allergen among children. They even have their own peanut-free table at school, where only approved lunches are allowed.

We cannot rely only on schools or other people. It's essential that we, as parents, are also aware and conscientious of our kids' friends with allergies and know what we should do in those situations.

The first thing you can do is to talk to the parents of those friends who have allergies to find out what they can and cannot eat and then stock up on goodies (see "The Plus or Minus Two Factor" section) with that information in mind.

Food Allergies 101

Here are five basic allergy facts and tips that every parent should know and use:

1. **Learn how to use an Epipen.** An Epipen is a "medical device used to deliver a measured dose (or doses) of epinephrine (also known as adrenaline) using auto injector technology, most frequently for the treatment of acute allergic reactions to avoid or treat the onset of anaphylactic shock."[12] If a child is too young or unable to administer the injection (which the child will most likely have on his or her person), it will be up to you to do the job.

2. **Know your ingredients.** Besides looking at food labels, be aware that many soaps, shampoos, and creams now use shea butter in their products, which comes from the shea nut. In other words, if your kids' friends are allergic to nuts, don't let them shower at your house or more likely wash their hands. Or you can just buy shampoo and soap without shea butter.

3. **Do your research on places to go.** Sporting arenas of any kind usually sell nuts in some form or another, especially baseball fields. The good news is that most Major League stadiums now have peanut-controlled zones. State fairs, concerts, and other events pose a similar risk, so if you're taking a child with you who suffers from allergies, make sure you are aware of everything around you and make smart decisions.

4. **Sharing is a no-no.** Sharing food and things like water bottles is not a good idea. You never know what the other person had to eat that may cause an allergic reaction to the person they are sharing with.

5. **Kissing.** Yep, it sounds pretty obvious, but if one person eats a peanut butter and jelly sandwich and then an hour later kisses someone who is allergic to peanuts, you could have a major problem on your hands—with the allergic reaction and the kissing.

HOW PREPARED ARE YOU?

1. Do you know which of your kids' friends have allergies and to what foods? Have you spoken to their parents about all of the details? What do they suggest you do to make your home a safe place for their child?

2. Based on that information, do an inventory of your pantry to determine what foods you should throw out or at least quarantine. By quarantine, I mean brightly labeled and placed with similar potentially hazardous foods but separated from other approved foods.

3. What else can you and your family do to protect those children?

4. Have a family meeting to discuss the changes you have made and to inform everyone on who, what, and why. It's important that everyone is not only aware but also an active member in the fight against allergic reactions at your home.

WILL WORK FOR PLAY

When I see the homeless on the side of the road holding up signs that say, "Will work for pay (or food)," I try to teach my children the value of this message, with an emphasis on the words "will work."

Unfortunately, due to an abundant life, my kids sometimes feel entitled to many things and have to be reminded that work is at the root of all we possess and enjoy. This is a difficult lesson for any parent to teach.

Mom: Angel, hurry up and clean your room, please. It's a mess.

Daughter (age five): No! I'm a princess, and princesses don't do that. They have servants who clean up after them.

Mom: You know you are not a real princess because your daddy isn't a real king?

Daughter: Well, the biggest mistake you ever made was not marrying a real king, because I'm cute and smart enough to be a real princess.

We have the same challenge in our family asking our four "princesses" to clean the kitchen. You would think they were Cinderella and that we were the mean stepmothers relegating them to a life of servitude without any chance of parole. The incessant whining, moaning, sighing, and exaggerated body language while doing the task often leads us to tell them to get lost so that we don't have to watch and listen to their sorry attitudes. In this, they win.

We have tried to teach the importance of cause and effect instead. "You work, and only then you play [or fill in the blank with whatever activity they cherish]." Here's a great example:

WANT TODAY'S WI-FI PASSWORD?
1. MAKE YOUR BEDS.
2. VACUUM DOWNSTAIRS.
3. WALK THE DOG.

When your children start bemoaning their fate, as they will do, remind them that it is your job to raise functioning citizens who understand that if they don't work, they don't get paid.

This reality was very apparent in my travels throughout India, where there is no government support or dole. If mothers, fathers, and, in many cases, children do not work, they do not get paid, which means they do not eat for the day. It's that simple.

To try and instill the value and importance of work in our children without shipping them off to India for a summer, we have tried to teach them the difference between rights and privileges. Rights are certain things all children deserve from their parents so that they can enjoy a normal, healthy childhood. Things like food, clothing, and love (remember Maslow's hierarchy of needs in the "Cows and Kids" section). Privileges, on the other hand, are things your children may think they can't live without but are not necessary for a normal and healthy childhood, such as buying a new sweater because it's cute, getting a smartphone because everyone has one, and so on. These privileges must be earned. And **BTW** (by the way), "You'll thank us when you have to look for a job one day," always elicits eye rolling and more complaints, but it's true. Knowing that we are right makes everything all right, and they will thank us one day.

The Stinky Sock Award

Start a new tradition by awarding the child with the longest streak for keeping their room clean (details **TBD** [to be determined] by you and kids)—the Stinky Sock Award. It's funny and irreverent—just how your kids like it.

TO LAUGH OR NOT TO LAUGH

As we have already determined, children can be embarrassing in public. But how we react to those children can be just as embarrassing to them. I've witnessed and personally tried two parenting approaches to these blushing moments—one effective and one ineffective.

The following effective example includes food, family, flatulence, and laughter. (I tried staying away from potty humor, but sometimes it accurately represents our realities the best because it's reality.)

The family of five had just sat down to eat lunch at a busy local restaurant. Beau, the nine-year-old son, was devouring his meatball sandwich after a grueling football practice when he scooted forward in the vinyl seats and let out the loudest wind imaginable. It was so loud that the entire restaurant turned and stared at Beau, his two brothers, and his embarrassed parents. The place went silent. It was as if someone had paused time. It was at this awkward moment that Mom and Dad could have jumped in and tried to save the situation, but luckily someone else in the family did.

Ben, Beau's younger brother, looked over at his brother and yelled, "That was the big kabooma!" Everyone erupted into laughter, and Beau and his poor parents were saved from a very uncomfortable silence by the unintentional but effective humor of a four-year-old. His parents, who had every right to scold their son, decided in that moment that laughter was the best way to parent. Only afterward, in private, did they talk to him about social consideration and manners.

There are also ineffective ways of dealing with embarrassing children and their embarrassing behaviors. One approach parents use is the "temporary orphan" parenting technique (see the previously mentioned section for more details), which really only works for the parent. Everyone else knows what happened and will keep staring, wondering if the parent really didn't see or hear what his or her kid just said or did.

Another ineffective technique is to yell and berate the child in public, which just makes everyone uncomfortable and feel bad for the child, and it is especially not good for the child. This is the worst response to an embarrassing child, who in many cases wasn't trying to embarrass you but was just expressing his or her thoughts and feelings.

I am an intense person. Certain things stress me out, especially when I am in public with my children. So choosing to laugh when things don't go as planned is not the easiest thing for me to do. I am learning, though. I may not be laughing yet—it's more of an uncomfortable grimace—but I am moving in that general direction. I now actually say a prayer and give myself a little pep talk before going anywhere with the Muller Mob: "Okay, fact: one of the kids is going to spill something, trip, cry, yell, fight, or embarrass me in some new and wonderful way. I will remain calm. I will shut my mouth, and I will smile. I will survive." I sincerely believe that one day I will progress to the stage where I genuinely laugh when I find myself in a stressful situation. I know it.

THE STESS-TO-LAUGHTER CONTINUUM

How about you? Where are you on the stress-to-laughter continuum? Do you need to give yourself a pep talk?

Please Note

Not every situation is a laughing matter, nor are there only two or three parenting approaches to dealing with embarrassing children. Some behaviors or situations are different or serious enough that they require a unique approach and action. This depends on you, your child, and the circumstance you find yourself in. Often you will not feel like laughing, nor will it be appropriate to do so. In those moments you will do what you have always done—go with your instinct or ask for help.

SILENCE SIGNALS SOMETHING

When Thomas Carlyle, the English poet, first translated the phrase "Silence is golden" in 1831 from the German novel *Sartor Resartus (The Tailor Retailored)*, he definitely didn't have parenting in mind.[13]

As parents, we may wish for, long for, and even pray for silence, but as we all know, it very rarely comes. And when it does come, it usually trumpets that something is wrong.

We did not recognize the silence before it was too late. The rest of the family was talking and playing together in the living room when my wife's sixth sense kicked in and she nervously asked, "Where are Gemma and TJ?" Before waiting for a response from us, Soni jumped up and instinctively moved to the area in the home that was suspiciously quiet, Gemma's room. On arrival, she let out a yelp. Not a scream of terror, but more like an involuntary expression of "What on earth happened here?" As we all made our way to see the cause of her concern, we were met with an art exhibition that only a four- and two-year-old could be the authors of: nail polish graffiti. Everywhere. Doors, drawers, closets, bedspreads, and floor. Nail polish has since been banned from our home.

You know your children. Rarely are they quiet unless they are asleep, especially if they are with another sibling or a friend. Even by themselves, they tend to talk to themselves or make relevant play sounds. Silence is typically an indication that something's up and that Junior or Missy is probably doing something he or she shouldn't be doing, like rubbing Vaseline all over his or her face, clothes, and your bedroom floor, or coating your new wood floor with cooking spray. Both true stories, but not with our kids this time, TY (Thank you) very much.

Unfortunately, the reality is that if you hear silence, it is probably too late anyway. What can you do to prevent similar disasters from happening to you? Probably nothing. Helicopter parenting is not a good option, and it will drive you bonkers anyway. However, you could check on your children more often. Who knows? You may be able to catch them in the act before they destroy something in your home. Besides that, you really can't do much about this parenting reality. Children are curious, and that is a good thing, even when it's a bad thing. Couches can be replaced, walls can be painted, and floors can be washed, but a child's imagination should be allowed to grow. Hopefully the canvas changes from walls to paper, though.

WELCOME BACK TO SCHOOL!

I overheard the following discussion between my daughter Ruby (in third grade) and her cousin (in second grade):

Cousin: My mom doesn't even know how to do first-grade math.

Ruby: Wow, that is so easy.

Cousin: Yup, she had to go online to learn it all over again, so she could teach me.

I don't know why we ever thought we were done with school when we graduated. What were we thinking? Like the mother in that story, we get to enjoy school all over again with each of our children—this time as the annoying and frustrated parent, the one that we promised ourselves we would never turn into.

I hope you find some of these back-to-school basics helpful in dealing with the back-to-school blues.

- **Back-to-School Basic #1: Hire a tutor if you can.** I don't know about you, but it has been a long time since I've done algebra. It will take more time for me to try and remember formulas and theories than it is worth. Save yourself and your children the headache and just pay someone else who knows what they are doing to help your children with homework. (If you cannot afford a tutor, then think of Basic #4 as your alternative.) Many junior high and high schools also offer before- and after-school peer and teacher tutoring free of charge. If you or your children are struggling with a subject, you may want to look into this as a possible solution.

- **Back-to-School Basic #2: Don't blame the teachers.** Most teachers are not the reason for your son's or daughter's poor grades. It's likely your child's fault for not putting enough time in or your fault for poor tutoring. There are obviously exceptions to this back-to-school reality, but before defaulting to blaming the teacher, start by looking at the effort and time your children are putting in to solving the problem. Don't we want our children to learn how to solve problems instead of being handed all the answers?

- **Back-to-School Basic #3: Take the updated sex education class yourself.** Seriously. These classes have changed a lot since you and I learned about the birds and the bees from hand-drawn slides of reproductive organs on the overhead projector. For many parents today, that was the extent of our sex education. That and having your best friend, Roger, show you his dad's dirty magazine. Unfortunately also a true story.

- **Back-to-School Basic #4: Take advantage of the millions of free learning fragments online and download the apps.** Use apps and online games and tools to teach your kids (and you) math and science. Quick drills, scoreboards, and badges are a great way for kids to learn an otherwise boring topic.

FAILURE *IS* AN OPTION

In life, especially in business settings, I've often heard the phrase "Failure is not an option."

IMO (in my opinion), this is a fallacy. Sometimes failure is the only option.

I remember watching my children as they learned how to walk. It was fascinating to see them progress from lying on their backs to rolling over, squirming forward, crawling, standing up, and then finally to taking that first glorious step. In every case, that first step was followed by a fall—and many more falls before they were walking confidently. Were all of those falls really failures?

How about learning to eat using a fork or spoon? Did your children get it right the first time? No. What about learning to read? Or speak? Or throw a ball? Or the thousand other things they have learned and will continue to learn in life? If they do not succeed at the first, second, or even the twentieth attempt, does this make them failures? Of course not. In almost all instances, success comes only after many failures.

We would never call those first baby steps and falls failures because we understand that they contributed to our children's growth and learning. So why, then, do we expect perfection right away in our children's other behaviors?

Unfortunately, our children are learning from our communities and society in general that failing is unacceptable. In oversized classrooms, they are expected to get it right the first time or they are out of luck. They take standardized tests that strip them of their unique gifts and talents so that every child fits the academic mold prescribed by a few. Then, based on those sterile scores, children are placed into categories where only the best are worthy to attend the best universities. Failure is not an option if you want to receive an Ivy League education. The reality is that some of our best and brightest children are branded as "not smart enough" from a young age because they do not fit the mold or standard. We beat the life and passion out of them so that we can have clean numbers and percentages. This reality then ripples into their careers and earning potential.

While we may not have a lot of influence on standardized testing, class sizes, or educational reform, we do have a direct influence on our children. That is the most important leverage point anyway because from the day they are born until the day they die, our children will look to us first for affirmation and support (even if it may not seem like it sometimes). We parents must be responsible stewards and teach our children that failure is acceptable as long as they learn from those experiences that not everyone wins at everything, that life is not always fair, that not everyone should receive a trophy, and that perfection may never be an option. If we honestly share these realities with them, while continuing to build them up and encourage them to try, they will be better suited to face life as an adult in the real world.

And whenever you doubt yourself, **PLS** (please) remember the wise words or Margaret Mead, an American cultural anthropologist, who said, "Never doubt that a small group of thoughtful, committed, citizens can change the world. Indeed, it is the only thing that ever has."[14] I ask you, what group of citizens is more important than parents?

Interesting Side Note

"Failure is not an option" is a phrase attributed to Gene Kranz, the NASA Mission Control flight director for the Apollo 13 space mission. While Mr. Kranz even wrote a book with that title, in reality he never actually used the phrase as indicated in the popular movie *Apollo 13*. The source of this pop culture phrase is in reference to an interview two of the scriptwriters for the movie had with the flight controller for the Apollo 13 mission, Jerry Bostick. During the interview, the writers asked Mr. Bostick, "Weren't there times when everybody, or at least a few people, just panicked?" His answer was simply, "No, when bad things happened, *we just calmly laid out all the options, and failure was not one of them*. We never panicked, and we never gave up on finding a solution." From this reply, the writers found inspiration and morphed two sentences into the now-famous line "Failure is not an option."[15]

TOUGHER THAN NAILS

When my oldest daughter was ten, we went on a rather challenging hike with her grandfather. We hiked the highest peak in Utah, King's Peak. With an elevation of 13,527 feet (4,123 meters) and a total round trip of around 26 miles (41.8 kilometers) in three days, this was not easy. Obviously I was a little apprehensive taking someone so young on such a difficult trip, but I knew her emotional maturity and physical fitness thanks to tennis and dance. While I must admit I had my doubts, I suspected she could do it, and I told her as much.

So we packed up our tents, sleeping bags, food, and water, and embarked on our journey. She nailed it, leaving many crying, whining Boy Scouts in her wake. Literally. I was the proudest father on the mountain as we confidently passed Scout after Scout on our way up. She was tougher physically than I had initially thought, and received many cheers and congratulations as we summited the peak.

In another, more serious example, I was raised in South Africa by a single mother in poor conditions. During a four- to five-year stretch, I remember moving and going to a different school every year. Because of this and other trying circumstances, I do not remember a single name of any of my teachers or of any friends during my early childhood years. Life was tough, but I was tougher. I was tougher emotionally than I thought I could be, and

I came out of a challenging upbringing relatively unscathed.

Children are survivors and always have been. While it is our duty as parents to protect our children as best we can from trauma, abuse, and experiences that could harm their future emotional and social state, we must be careful not to stunt their toughness and growth by being too overprotective or controlling. There is strength in adversity, and, trust me, our children will have enough tough times to test their toughness, if you allow them to be tested. I am not saying we should create emotional and social dilemmas that would scar them for life. What I am saying is that when life happens, use those teaching moments to persuade, sculpt, and toughen up, not baby, spoil, and control.

Providing opportunities for our children to toughen up is another parenting reality that requires balance, which we all know is sometimes hard to find—especially considering that every situation and child demands a different and unique approach in order to find that balance. Like most of the reality parenting principles in this book, my goal with this one isn't to propose one surefire solution but rather to raise your awareness about this principle and encourage you to take appropriate action based on your parenting situation.

PREPARE TO BE SURPRISED

When is comes to parenthood, the one thing you can be absolutely certain of is that your children will surprise you in the most wonderful and peculiar ways imaginable.

Let's start with the *wonderful* ways our children can surprise us. An elderly man moved into a rundown home down the street from us that needed a lot of work. One night Soni and I were talking about some of his health issues and what we could do to help him with the house and in general. Among other ideas, Soni suggested we invite him to dinner at least once a week, and I thought mowing his lawn would be helpful because his knees and back were giving him trouble. What we didn't realize was that one of our children was listening in on our conversation and decided to take on the responsibility herself.

The next day, to our pleasant surprise, she recruited two of her friends, went down to our new neighbor's house, and proceeded to mow his lawn and weed his garden. The three friends did this consistently throughout the summer, teaching their parents a valuable lesson about the importance of involving their children in their service endeavors.

As I researched stories for this book, service was the one theme that kept surfacing. Parents shared experience after experience about how their children surprised them with breakfast in bed, cleaning the house, doing the laundry without being asked, and a dozen other small but significant acts. This should come as no surprise to us. It is in children's genes to be good and do good. It's only when they grow up that they become tainted by the world and lose some of that purity and innocence.

Now on to some of the *strange* and *peculiar* surprises. Like the witty son who metaphorically stated, "Mom, these pants are too tight! They make me feel like a grown-up tiger stuck in a baby tiger's fur!"

Or the thoughtful daughter who responded to her mother's plea to "Hurry and get your shoes on!" with, "Mom, not now. I've got a date with destiny."

Or the son who put forth a good argument as well as some sound reasoning with, "You know, I've been having showers for a long time now, so I think it's probably time that I can quit."

Or the smart three-year-old daughter who was taking the

batteries out of the TV remote so that she could "put [the battery] in our doggy's ears because he doesn't listen to me."

Or the proper little lady who surprised herself by tooting and said, "How can that horrible smell come from a sweet little girl like me?"

Or the imaginative son who told his mother he thought she was a vampire because "you have lightning speed. One second you're in the kitchen, and then all of a sudden you are right next to me."

Life as a parent is anything but dull. Just open your eyes and your ears and prepare to be amazed . . . and surprised.

Ain't life wonderful?

NOTES

1.   Dr. Haim Ginott, *Between Parent and Child: The Bestselling Classic That Revolutionized Parent-Child Communication*, rev. upd. ed. (New York: Three Rivers Press, 2003).

2.   A. H. Maslow, "A Theory of Human Motivation," *Psychological Review* 50 no. 4 (1943): 370–96, http://psychclassics.yorku.ca/Maslow/motivation.htm.

3.   Elva Anson, *How to Get Kids to Help at Home* (Fair Oaks, CA: Emidra Publishing, 2004).

4.   Wikipedia, s.v. "The birds and the bees," last modified January 18, 2014, http://en.wikipedia.org/wiki/The_birds_and_the_bees.

5.   "Talking to Your Young Child About Sex," American Academy of Pediatrics, last modified July 9, 2013, http://www.healthychildren.org/English/ages-stages/preschool/pages/Talking-to-Your-Young-Child-About-Sex.aspx.

6.   *Forrest Gump*, directed by Robert Zemeckis (1994), DVD.

7.   "National Survey on American Attitudes on Substance Abuse XVII: Teens," CASA Columbia, last modified August 2012, http://www.casacolumbia.org/templates/NewsRoom.aspx?articleid=692&zoneid=51.

8.   Tristam Stuart, *Waste: Uncovering the Global Food Scandal* (New York: Penguin, 2009), http://www.feeding5k.org/food-waste-facts.php#sthash.zyvwbA6B.dpuf.

9.   Deborah Smith Pegues, *30 Days to Taming Your Tongue: What You Say (and Don't Say) Will Improve Your Relationships* (Eugene, OR: Harvest House Publishers, 2005).

10.   *The State of Food and Agriculture* (Food and Agriculture Association of the United Nations, 2013), http://www.fao.org/docrep/018/i3300e/i3300e.pdf.

11.   Ruchi S. Gupta, et al., "The Prevalence, Severity and Distribution of Childhood Food Allergy in the United States," *Pediatrics* (June 20, 2011). doi: 10.1542/ped.2011-0204.

12.   Wikipedia, s.v. "Epinephrine autoinjector," last modified January 18, 2014, http://en.wikipedia.org/wiki/Epinephrine_autoinjector.

13.   Thomas Carlyle, *Sartor Resartus (1831)* and *Lectures on Heroes (1840)* (London: Chapman & Hall, 1863).

14.   Margaret Mead, *Continuities in Cultural Evolution*, (New Haven, CT: Yale University Press, 1964).

15.   "Origin of *Apollo 13* Quote: 'Failure is not an Option,'" last modified January 11, 2013, http://www.spaceacts.com/notanoption.htm.

4. THE REALITY OF PARENTING TEENS

NO ONE IS EXEMPT

Once you've given birth to a child, that child will inevitably become a teenager. It's just how things work. As a parent, you cannot skip the teen years or apply some magical balm to lessen the effect it will have on your emotional well-being.

Some parents around the world try to bypass these years by sending their adolescent kids away to boarding school. Others, like my father, choose to quit family life and leave, only to reappear after the teen years have passed. But those are not honorable or viable options. You cannot run away from your teenager, but you can face the realities head on while looking forward to the day they grow out of whatever it is that teenagers go through.

For those of you who are sitting with a smug look on your face and thinking, "You are wrong about this one. My teenage son or daughter has been really good and has not given me problems," there is an added wrinkle you may not have thought of: even if your child is close to perfect, I can guarantee their friends will not be. To one degree or another, you'll still be living with the dreaded teenage years. No, you are not exempt either.

ME, MYSELF, AND ME AGAIN

There is a peculiar transformation that occurs with all kids. Even though it is expected, it is still a little unnerving when it happens. I am referring to the metamorphosis of our sweet and kind young children into irritable, self-centered teens seemingly overnight. Smiles decrease, yelling increases, and with it comes a general feeling of unhappiness and pessimism. This is what I call IBS, or irritable boy syndrome (also prevalent in girls but IGS isn't as catchy as IBS because this acronym also stands for irritable bowel syndrome).

After all, life for most teenagers is all about them. The earth and the solar system literally revolve around them. This is natural. It's part of maturing and establishing an identity in the world.

I remember watching this odd phenomenon transpire right before my eyes. It seemed that the calm and happy preteen turned into a teen who was constantly rolling his eyes and saying, "Mom (or Dad), you are sooooo annoying." I found this so amusing that I recorded him saying that phrase and then used a cool app on my phone to make a rap song out of it. Luckily, he found it funny too. The good news is that this teen seems to have outgrown his IBS.

Yes, adolescence equals drama and irritability regardless of gender. It is partly the result of your teens having to deal with the onslaught of puberty, acne, and a whole new batch of emotions, puberty, and acne. It occurred when you and I were young, and it will inevitably happen with your teenagers.

During these years, you will likely also get "the look"—the one that emits a lot of anger and frustration. If looks could kill, all parents would be dead, but, fortunately, it doesn't. Your children will hate you at times and say so through words, behaviors, and their eyes. It's a reality. There is no cure, technique, or solution for this reality, especially since each adolescent has his or her own strain of this virus.

Don't hate them back. Remember, to react this way is natural, and requires self-control on your part. I really struggle with this one. My advice would be to accept that there will be drama and don't react to it. Don't take it personally. If possible, separate yourself from the drama emotionally and, in some instances, physically. Since there is a good chance that there is no logical reason for what you are witnessing try not to make sense of it. Just remain calm and walk away.

Not much more to say about this reality except good luck and don't give up. One day the light will go on in your teenager's head, and he or she will realize that it's only when they look outside of themselves that they will truly find themselves. For some, that beautiful revelation comes sooner than others. When it does come, it is amazing to witness. Your "me" monster will no longer be preoccupied with only him- or herself but also will be committed to helping others, serving strangers, and sacrificing for friends, family, and neighbors. In our culture we call this maturing, but it is more than that; it is the germination of wisdom, the expression of unconditional love, and the discovery of true self.

TWO TRIPS IN TIME

You may have moments when you feel like you need to get away. Like when you hear "I hate you" from a child. In *Mom Rules*, I suggested that when you hear those three hurtful words to think of them as a compliment. However, in the moment when you are receiving this magnanimous compliment from a child who is literally foaming at the mouth and has smoke coming out of her ears, you may not feel like this statement is coming from a place of love and admiration.

But this is exactly when you should try, if possible, to separate yourself from the emotion of the moment and take two trips in your mental time machine. Its going to be tricky to take these trips and still stay connected to what is going on in the conversation, so you may want to sincerely ask for a moment of silence so that you can think. Pausing before reacting is actually a good practice in any emotionally charged discussion. That way you won't say something you will regret. Needless to say, this is going to be a hard reality to navigate. Good luck.

First, transport yourself back to when you where a teenager. Yes, I know how painful that experience was. I also remember battling acne, puberty, an out-of-whack body, and social awkwardness all at once. But also try to remember how frustrated you were at times with your parents—or anyone in authority, for that matter. Did you really hate that person? Can you even remember the details surrounding a single experience when you felt like you hated your parents? Unless it was an experience in which a parent behaved badly and scarred you for life, you probably don't have many memories. Even if you can recall hating your parents, did those feelings last very long? Probably not. The point here is that your child will get over the way they feel about you, especially if you don't react negatively to their outburst.

The second trip you need to try to take is into the future. Imagine your child as a functioning adult and maybe even a parent. How would you want that child to parent? What type of example should you set in that exact moment? Think of him or her thanking you for being consistent in your discipline and unconditional in your love and care.

Now, back to reality and the unhappy child in front of you. Both of these trips in time should make you smile. Not a patronizing grin but a genuine, peaceful smile. And since a sincere smile does not reflect the anger and frustration being projected onto you by your son or daughter, it may even alleviate some of the tension of the moment. At least it is a good place to start.

After a run-in with my emotionally out-of-control teen one night, I practiced what I preach and took these two trips in time and did not react or to mirror her frustrations. I was pleasantly surprised to find her back to normal the next morning without any trace of her previous frustrations. Sometimes kids just need some space and time to figure things out themselves.

One mother shared that when she hears "I hate you," she responds by flashing a big, genuine smile, clapping her hands, and saying, "Wonderful! My job is to raise a child that does as I have done and improves upon what he received." She takes it a step further by giving her child a blank journal and encouraging him to record all the things he will do differently when he is a parent. While this may not fly with all children, she knew it would with hers, and then she created a great teaching opportunity.

TECHNOLOGICAL SELF-ASSESSMENT (TSA)

Before attempting to bridge the digital divide over the next few sections, let's see how tech-savvy and social-media smart you really are. Place a check mark next to all the statements that apply to you. Then add up all the check marks and refer to the scoring key to find out how you're doing.

- ☐ You have taken a picture of something interesting or funny just so that you can share it with your Facebook or other social media friends.
- ☐ You own a smartphone and know how to use it.
- ☐ You have a Twitter handle and know how to use a hashtag (#).
- ☐ You have been on a Google Hangout.
- ☐ You monitor your children's social media and gaming activity frequently.

☐ You have had a conversation with one person while texting another.

☐ You have good filters set up on your home computers.

☐ You know what video games your children play and what they are rated.

☐ You have used YouTube to learn something new.

☐ You use Instagram as your family's scrapbook by printing books from your account (or from another social media site).

☐ You have created a Facebook page for your business, product, band, book, art, a cause, or your community.

☐ You have repinned something from Pinterest.

☐ You have spoken to your children about the risks and dangers of pornography.

☐ You have geotagged a post or pin.

☐ You have contributed to a wiki of one kind or another (for example, Wikipedia).

☐ You frequently read someone else's blog.

☐ You have used the parental controls on your TV to lock specific channels and shows.

☐ You have asked your online friends or connections for a service they'd recommend for a problem you are faced with (for example, the name of a good plumber).

☐ You browse your Facebook news feed at least once a day.

☐ You have clear rules on cell phone use, television watching, and gaming in your family.

Key:

0–3: You are in serious need of a major technological update. Pay close attention to this section in the book and hire a teenager to tutor you now, and hopefully you will stand a chance.

4–9: You are making progress, but you still have a long

way to go. You should also pay attention to this section.

10–15: Well done. You are probably considered "cool" by your children's friends and annoying by your own children. There are still some principles in this section you can learn from.

16–20: Congratulations! You are officially a social media nerd and a tech- savvy parent. You have the smarts to know what is going on in the social sphere. Look for things you don't know about yet in this section.

(This TSA is adapted from one I used in the business book I coauthored, *The Learning Explosion: 9 Rules to Ignite Your Virtual Classroom*)

RATED "M" FOR "MOMMA-APPROVED"

Have you taken the time lately to actually stand behind your children as they played video games? You may be surprised at what you see.

Do any of these games look or sound familiar? *Carmageddon, Heavy Rain, Soldier of Fortune, God of War II, Gears of War 2, Mortal Kombat, Dante's Inferno, Thrill Kill, Dragon Age: Origins, MadWorld, Manhunt, Postal 2, and Grand Theft Auto.*

If you were to watch your young impressionable child play any of these games listed, you may be surprised and shocked to see him (or her) orchestrating gangland-style beat downs, participating in gang rapes, barbecuing prostitutes with flamethrowers, using cat carcasses as silencers on your gun, hitting people with anthrax-laden cow heads, having sex in nightclubs, back rooms, cars, and playing "fetch" with dogs using the severed heads of your dismembered victims. And this is just a small sampling of the types of behaviors and scenarios you can find in some "games." Most parents probably don't want their kids to learn how to kill, solicit sex, and buy drugs, but this is exactly what some games teach them to do.

If you are like me, you probably grew up with video games like Donkey Kong and Mario Bros. These were entertaining and safe. But many parents still think, incorrectly, that the video games their children play today are similar to these classics. Unfortunately, some of the recent popular smartphone games like *Angry Birds*, *Farmville*, and *Temple Run* have reinforced the incorrect paradigm that games are still games and are perfectly safe. That's because these and many other games like them *are* still good and safe.

The truth is both sobering and frightening. Hundreds of games are not suited for children. Most parents would never allow their children to watch a television show or movie depicting pornographic scenes, killing sprees, and drug trafficking, yet they ignorantly allow their children to play games that have all of those scenarios and more. Don't underestimate the graphic images and adult content found in some games. Just because it's called a game doesn't mean there isn't real danger.

According to experts too much screen time can be detrimental to your child's physical and emotional health. The American Psychiatric Association, found that children who played violent video games have significantly higher feelings of aggression and differences in brain activity during both cognitive motor activity and resting periods.[1] And a recent Harris Poll survey found that almost one in ten children that play video games is addicted.[2]

The American Academy of Pediatrics (AAP) recommends that kids under age two have no screen time and that kids older than two watch no more than one to two hours a day of quality programming.[3] Note the word "quality." In other words, limiting the screen time your child is not sufficient. You must also monitor that time to ensure it is quality, or Momma-approved.

For help knowing what to look out for, go to the Entertainment Software Rating Board for a list of all of the ratings and what they mean.[4] They start with "eC" for "Early Childhood," and then "E" for "Everyone," all the way up to "M" for "Mature" and "A" for "Adults Only." Always check the rating of the games your kids play and, even then, be a little more conservative than suggested. Even rating boards are fairly subjective. Only once Mom has watched a game and given her final "Momma-approved" stamp should the children be allowed to play it.

REALITY CHECK

GAMING

It may be advantageous for you to ask yourself the following questions:

- Do you know what games your kids have?

- What are their games rated?

- Have you ever played (or watched) the games your kids play? If not, plan on spending a night with the gamers.

- How many hours do you allow your children to play a week?

- If you do not have a limit already, when will you lay down the law?

- How will you hold them accountable for following the law?

THE NEW BEST FRIEND

Your child's new best friend may not be who you think it is. Think of the thing your kids spend the most time with, even when they are sitting next to their other best friend, Jane or Johnny. Yes, it's their mobile device. That's the reality for many children today.

According to a Generation M2 study conducted by the Henry J. Kaiser Family Foundation, children spend more time consuming media on their cell phones than actually talking on them.[5] The study also revealed that parents have a major influence on their children's media use. For example, children whose parents limit their media use (by setting household rules) do, in fact, spend less time with media than their peers. They also go on to do better in school than their peers. In other words, if parents get involved in their kids' media consumption, their kids will be better off in the long run.

But beyond the limits you set, you and your spouse also set an example for you children. I recently caught my wife and myself using our cell phones on a date recently instead of talking to each other. Having the world at your fingertips is a tempting proposal for most human beings, but we have to bring back the humanity. As parents, we are raising the next generation, and, if we are not careful, they will be the silent generation—heads down, fingers engaged, and never talking face to face with their fellow human beings. I know I sound like a doomsayer, but it really is getting bad.

The key is to establish clear rules for what is and is not appropriate cell phone use. For example, our children are not allowed to pull out their cell phones at any family event—dinner, birthdays, and so on. The consequence? Confiscated cell phone for an agreed-upon duration. The only way this works is if we adhere to the same rules as well. Otherwise, our hypocritical behavior will only cause contention and dissension.

We will allow exceptions to the rule if approved beforehand. For example, someone is expecting an important call (importance must also be defined beforehand) during an aforementioned family event.

REALITY CHECK

WHAT ARE THE RULES?

1. Can your children take their phones to bed?

2. When can they use their cell phones?

3. When are they *not* allowed to use their cell phones?

4. What are the consequences for breaking the rules?

5. Is there a text limit? Data limit? What are the consequences for going over the limits?

THE NEW BULLY ON THE BLOCK

Sometimes parents make life harder than it should be by giving us names, like Treion, that just beg to be teased. Treion is not a common name, even in South Africa where I was born and raised, but it does rhyme with "pee on" wherever English is spoken. Kids pick up on this. Actually, rhyming names with offensive terms and phrases is one of the first levels of bullying because it is easy to do at almost any age. "Pee on the Treion" was a phrase I heard a lot growing up, but it usually ended after I leveled the ringleader of the group, which in my case didn't lead to ongoing bullying. But that isn't the case with the thirteen million kids who are the victims of bullying in the United States today.[6]

According to the stopbullying.gov definition, bullying is "unwanted, aggressive behavior among school-aged children that involves a real or perceived power imbalance. The behavior is repeated, or has the potential to be repeated, over time. Bullying includes actions such as making threats, spreading rumors, attacking someone physically or verbally, and excluding someone from a group on purpose."[7]

I have a friend who was born with a cleft lip and was the victim of severe bullying throughout his life. He shared the following experience with me: "During my sophomore year in high school, I showed up to my regular table, where I ate lunch with whom I thought were close friends, to find them all laughing at a picture one of them had drawn. It was a picture of me and my mom having oral sex. Our names were written above our faces so every one knew it was me. Because I was upset by that and 'couldn't take a joke,' these so-called friends began spreading rumors about me in and out of school."

Luckily, he was able to survive these years of incredible hurt and torment. Since then, he has been able to help and support his own son, who was also the victim of bullying at school.

And if bullying in the schoolyard isn't hard enough, we now have the Internet and social media to complicate matters. A recent review of the research found 15 to 35 percent of students have been victims, and 10 to 20 percent admit to engaging in cyberbullying.[8]

Cyberbullying can come in the form of text messages, pictures, videos via mobile phone cameras, social media posts, phone calls, emails, online chat rooms, instant messaging (IM), and through actual websites. And due to continual technological advances, the list of ways children will be bullied in the future will continue to grow.

The consequences of bullying in all its ugly categories can be seen all around us. Our children are committing suicide at an alarming rate due to what is happening to them in person and online. According to the Centers for Disease Control and Prevention, suicide is the third leading cause of death in kids ages fifteen to twenty-four, and suicide attempts have risen from 6.3 percent in 2009 to 7.8 percent in 2011.[9] As parents, it's our responsibility to protect our children from all perceived and real dangers. We can do this in three ways:

1. **Be awake and aware.** Your child may not verbally communicate to you that he or she is the victim of bullying in any of its forms. However, you know your children. You know when something is wrong. But sometimes, in order for you to see through the smoke and mirrors that your magician teen puts up to hide his or her reality, you have to be awake and present in your teen's life. If you haven't realized this yet, parenting is a full-time job. It's hard work, and no one else can do it.

2. **Have real talks.** Life gets busy, but having frequent one-on-one talks with each child is essential to the health of you and your child's relationship (Dad Rule #67). Real communication is informal, sincere, and patient, and it takes time.

3. **Stay connected.** I talk about this in more depth in the next section, but the parenting principle here is to be

involved and connected with your child on every level, including social media. Even if you are just the silent observer on FB (Facebook), you may be able to recognize the signs of bullying sooner.

Incidentally, I didn't learn from my parents' mistakes either, because I ended up naming my only son after me. However, he has been called TJ (Treion Junior) since he was born, so hopefully he isn't the victim of teasing or bullying because of it.

BEING A WATCHDOG

Ask yourself the following three questions to determine whether you are doing what you need to protect your child from bullying and cyberbullying:

1. Am I fully present in body and mind in my children's lives?

2. Do I conduct frequent one-on-one talks with my children?

3. Am I connected to them on all social media sites?

SOCIALLY SMART, SAVVY, AND SAFE

Follow, *like*, and *hang out* all mean different things today. These are all social media terms that you should not only be familiar with but actively practicing with your children, because this is how they are communicating and interacting with friends and strangers alike. With the proliferation of social media like Facebook, Twitter, Google Plus, and mainstream media tools, it has never been more imperative for parents to be connected to their children online.

Be Social Media Smart

You can learn a lot about your kids by what they post on social media sites. Think about it. They are generally much more open with their friends than they are with you, so being connected with your kids will allow you to be the proverbial fly on the wall. It will also alert you to potentially embarrassing moments and behavioral issues.

According to teens, parents who use social media are more likely to talk with their teen about what kinds of things should and should not be shared online or on a cell phone. Teens report that parents who are friends with their teens on social media are more likely to have these conversations than parents who have not "friended" their child (92 percent versus 79 percent).[10]

SOCIAL MEDIA CRASH COURSE

Want to know what all the newfangled social media hoopla is all about? Start by learning what these key terms mean.

TWEET. This is a reference to *what* you do on Twitter—sending a short message into the world for those that follow you to read. A tweet is also referred to as a microblog because each tweet can only be 140 characters (including spaces) long but can contain a link to a website, article, or anything else on the web.

TWITTER HANDLE. A handle is the same as your Twitter username (fifteen characters), not to be confused with your real name (twenty characters), which also shows up under your handle in your profile.

FOLLOWERS. You are a follower if you choose to "like" someone's Facebook page, "follow" someone on Twitter or Pinterest, and subscribe to someone's blog or website.

BLOG. A blog is simply how people keep a journal online today. Bloggers are those who author these family and business websites. Many "mommy bloggers" have made a fortune by accruing a bunch of followers and then selling advertising space to the highest bidders and top name brands.

HANGOUT. Google Plus is a social media site where friends and professionals can hold online conversations using photos, emoticons (icons depicting emotions, like a smiley face), video cameras, and instant messaging (similar to Skype).

PIN. Pinterest has taken the online world by storm. In a unique approach to sharing, pinners can post photos, pictures, art, infographics, or anything visual on the web. People then choose which pinners to follow and repin the images of those they follow on their own Pinterest news feed.

SHARE. You've probably noticed the word "share" on most websites. This simply allows you, the visitor, to share that specific web page with your followers and friends on the social media site of your choice.

NEWSFEED. Almost all social media sites have a newsfeed, and it is not a banner like you see on ESPN or CNN showing the latest scores or news. Rather it is a real-time, ongoing feed of all the people you follow, showing you the news of their lives.

BEING SOCIALLY SAVVY

Besides being connected, parents can engage in several other practices to protect their children in the online world. The following best practices apply to you as well as your children:

1. **Educate yourself and your children on the risks of putting yourself "out there."** We really do live in a huge world, especially when we can connect with someone across the globe instantaneously. The more information you post about yourself, where you live, how old you are, and what you like to do, the greater the likelihood that you or your children could receive unwanted advances, have your identity stolen, or have your privacy violated. I'm not saying you shouldn't network and join social media sites, but be aware of the risks.

2. **Be careful what you post.** Many job recruiters nowadays will do a Google search on all job applicants. So realize that all viewpoints, texts, and media that you have posted regarding your political views, sexual orientation, personal shenanigans, profanity, poor grammar, or inappropriate photos or videos are now permanently part of your personal portfolio, whether you like it or not. You don't have to look far to find politicians and celebrities who have been embarrassed in the media because they violated this rule. Their exploits, usually sexual in nature, are all over the news and Internet. Once you click "done" or "enter" or "share," it is gone for good. So think before you act.

3. **Explore the social media site before giving permission for your children to join.** Find out if a profile is

117

required, what the privacy settings are, how to delete an account, and who owns your content. It's important to know if the website can share or resell your personal information, photos, and content with third parties. Also find out how you and your children can report inappropriate content and unwanted contact.

4. **Be picky about your "friends" and who you are connected to.** Ensure that you have the same friends as your children if at all possible so that you can see what they see. Together with your child, remove friends who you feel are not good influences and discuss in detail why what they said, posted, or messaged was not acceptable.

5. **Establish clear rules on what can and cannot be shared or posted on any site.** This principle also related back to the "The Teenager Agreement" section on page 132. For example, make sure everyone involved, including you, knows that posting scantily clad pictures and provocative posts of any kind are not allowed. I would also recommend you read the "Six Degrees of Dumb" section on page 64 and talk to you kids about what family information they can and cannot share (the second Degree of Dumb).

6. **Listen to what others are saying about you and your children.** Being vigilant and aware will help you catch cyberbullying and other potentially harmful behaviors before they get out of hand.

7. **Protect the privacy of others.** You also have the responsibility to ensure that your child is not responsible for

sharing offensive and hurtful information about others. Do not allow your children to be bullies in any way.

8. **Optional practice.** If you feel your children need this added level of protection and supervision, you may require that you know all your children's usernames and passwords. Then you might frequently sign in as them and peruse their messages and newsfeeds so that you can intercept any potentially harmful situations and inappropriate content.

It is always good practice to protect yourself and your children from potential social media identify theft by using strong passwords. At some point, you will need to trust your children and allow them to have their own accounts, because if you don't give your permission, they will just create their own private accounts anyway. When that should happen is between you and them. My recommendation would be to follow the specific restrictions provided by most social media sites. Facebook, for example, only allows users who are thirteen years of age or older to sign up for an account. Knowing your child, you may feel differently about what age you want them to be unleashed into the World Wide Web.

BUY IT SO YOU CAN CONTROL IT

Here is a parenting principle that if followed in the right spirit can solve a lot of parenting woes—buy it so you can control who uses it and for how long.

The Counterargument

I know there will many that will disagree with me on this point and mention all the valuable lessons children can learn by saving up for something and then being responsible owners. I humbly suggest we **A2D** (agree to disagree). I believe certain modern-day things, if not moderated carefully, will adversely affect children, and that many children do not have the life experiences or self discipline to be responsible owners of these possessions . . . yet.

They will watch or play as much as they possibly can if not kept in check. Without a fence to keep them in, our children will continue to roam. The reality is that many parents today are so busy with careers and life in general that we do not set appropriate boundaries or hold our children accountable to those boundaries. So if you want your children to learn the value of saving up for something they want, have them save up to be a partial owner with you being the majority owner. In this way they still benefit by saving but are not given carte-blanche access. You still hold veto rights if the agreed-upon time or use is violated.

Caleb knows he can only play two hours of video games today. Sarah knows that if she exceeds her text limit, her phone will be taken for a month. Katie knows that she must return her mother's iPad to her when she has finished watching the movie or playing *Temple Run* or she will not able to use the iPad for a week. Why do these teenagers know the restrictions on these digital devices? Because all the devices belong to their parents, and they have a clear agreement on how long they can spend on a device and what the consequences are for breaking that agreement.

Be Clear on the Rules

Remember those violent and mature video games? Never allow your kids to buy them, because then they think they have the right to play them when they want. Make a fast rule that only you can buy video games. That way you know what is coming into your home, and you can stop anything inappropriate before it comes through the front door. You could even joke with your kids that your gaming avatar name is "The Gatekeeper."

The same principle applies to cell phones. We bought our daughter a cell phone and immediately spoke to her about when and how much she could use it. For example, if we call her and she doesn't pick up or call us back within five minutes, she forfeits the right to use the phone for a week. Why so harsh? Well, the main reason for giving her a phone is so that we can stay in contact with her. If the phone is not being used for its primary purpose, what use is it? Obviously, we will not punish her if she has a legitimate excuse or reason, like she was playing in a soccer game or watching a movie. Communication clears up most confusion.

We have also made an agreement that cell phones are not to be used during family dinners and events (unless there is a real need). Consequences are more severe when this rule is broken—one month without the phone. Family time is that important to us. Again, we are not so strict that we will not listen to reason, but having clear rules and consequences sure makes those discussions easier.

When should your children get their own phones? This is not an easy question to answer. You have to consider all of the pros and cons and weigh them with what you know about your children. Do you want the convenience of staying in touch with them anytime, anywhere? Do you trust them? Will they use their phones safely by not texting or sharing private information with strangers? Most important, ask yourself if your children actually *need* rather than *want* a phone. Some children can be trusted from a young age to own a cell phone; others may need to mature more and prove they can be trusted with the responsibility of owning one.

Limit Usage

Limiting tech use—texting, gaming, watching, playing—in some families may start a third world war unless mutually agreed-upon rules are established up front. And even then there may be minor skirmishes, attempted stealth operations, and sulking parties. This is normal. Stick to your battle plan, and all will turn out fine.

You know your kids are growing up in a digital world when they ask you if you could change the beeping noise on the microwave to a different ringtone. This should come as no surprise if you look at how much our kids are immersed in technology. As a matter of fact, kids ages eight to eighteen now spend an *average* of ten hours and forty-five minutes a day, seven days a week with media. That translates into seventy-five hours and fifteen minutes per week, nearly twice as many hours as their parents put into full-time jobs.[11]

This is way too much. The Center for Internet Addiction Recovery and the Video Game Addiction Organization identified potential warning signs for children with pathological Internet use.[12] I have included these warning signs in the following Reality Check.

WARNING SIGNS OF COMPULSIVE INTERNET USE

You know your child has a problem when you can see the following behaviors from him or her. Check all that apply.

- Preoccupation with the Internet or specific Internet destinations.

- Defensive about time spent online.

- Spends money on their devices or online that should be used for bills, groceries, and other necessities.

- Failed attempts to control behavior, including aggressive behavior.

- A heightened sense of euphoria while involved in computer and Internet activities.

- Loses track of time while online.

- Sacrifices needed hours of sleep to spend time online.

- Becomes agitated or angry when not online or when online time is interrupted.

- Checks messages compulsively throughout the day.

- Spends time online in place of homework or chores.

- Prefers to spend time online rather than with friends or family.

- Disobeys time limits that have been set for Internet usage.

- Lies about amount of time spent online or sneaks online when no one is around.

- Seems preoccupied with getting back online when away from the computer.

- Loses interest in activities that were enjoyable before he or she had online access.

- Escapes into the Internet to avoid responsibilities or to escape painful feelings or troubling situations.

- Depression.

If you believe your child is a compulsive user or even an addict, several organizations and clinics can help. Start your search by typing "Internet addiction recovery" or "video game addiction" in your browser and then reach out to the relevant resource.

PORNOGRAPHY IS IN YOUR HOME

When I was growing up, the only way pornography could find its way into your home was if you physically carried it in the form of a magazine or book or VHS tape. As you know, things have changed a lot since then. Today, porn creeps into everyone's home through wireless routers, telephone lines, cell phone networks, and various high-tech cables and wires. It may not be activated yet, but sometimes all it takes is typing in one word in a browser window to open up a whole other world you don't want your kids to discover.

I was typing the web address of a popular non-pornographic website in my browser window when, to my surprise, up came an explicit porno page. After quickly closing down the window,

I looked at my browsing history to see what I had done wrong. I had misspelled the name by one letter, and the funny thing was that the misspelled name wasn't even a proper word. It was as if the porn industry was buying domain names with common misspellings of popular websites so that they could attract new and unsuspecting visitors. At first I was not sure if my unscientific presumption was true, but then I did a little research and discovered that it is actually common for pornographers to do this exact thing. Another tactic of these back-alley marketers is to buy domain names of popular expired domains and then redirect that URL name to one of their porn sites. In fact, this practice is so common it even has a name, "porn-napping." In other words, your child may be on a G-rated princess website one day and then log in the next day to find the princess has lost all her innocence and virtue. This happened to Ernst and Young's popular children's money management site Moneyopolis. Due to a clerical oversight, the domain name expired and was quickly snatched up by porn-nappers, who redirected unsuspecting visitors to a sexually explicit site. FYI (for your information), the name was bought back, but at a hefty price. Ernst and Young are not the only victims of porn-napping; even the U.S. Department of Education once became a porn site overnight.[13]

Has this ever happened to you or, even worse, to one of your children? You are not alone. According to a report, 34 percent of Internet users have experienced unwanted exposure to pornographic content through ads, pop-up ads, misdirected links or emails.[14]

That is one-third of all Internet users!

I also came to the disturbing realization that pornography is easier to access than *Scooby-Doo*. Yes, this statement may seem dramatic, but it's still true. To watch *Scooby-Doo* or almost any other family-appropriate entertainment online, you may have to pay a monthly fee to a streaming service like Netflix or Hulu. However, anyone can find free porn to watch. This is a reality that you not only need to be aware of but one in which you need to take action. What are you going to do about it?

Filters Are a Pain in the Butt but Essential

The first reality parenting principle you can apply is to get a good filter for your home computers. I am the first to say how annoying it is to have a functioning filter on a computer. I hate having to type my password in for every click I make on some websites, like Facebook. However, this means that worse sites are *not* getting through to my kids, and they are not part of the 34 percent of Internet users that are accidently exposed to inappropriate material. In my opinion, that is worth the extra clicks, password entries, and few extra dollars.

While you can pay for very good filters, you can also download some free versions. While you don't have to spend the *money*, you should spend the *time* finding the right one that works for you and our family. In case you needed any more motivation on this topic, here are some more sobering statistics:

- Teenagers with frequent exposure to sexual content on TV have a substantially greater likelihood of teenage pregnancy, and the likelihood of teen pregnancy was twice as high when the quantity of sexual content exposure within the viewing episodes was high.[15]

- Pornography viewing by teens disorients them during the developmental phase when they have to learn how to handle their sexuality and when they are most vulnerable to uncertainty about their sexual beliefs and moral values.[16]

- A significant relationship also exists among teens between frequent pornography use and feelings of loneliness, including major depression.[17]

Keep Up with Technology, Even if It Is Scary

While I realize there are many parents who are tech savvy and leading the online charge, there are some of you who are still on the outside looking in. If you have ever referred to the Internet as the "Interweb," then I am talking to you.

I hope by now I have persuaded you fence-sitters to get in the game, literally. You've been introduced to the violent and sexually explicit games kids are playing nowadays, read how technology has proliferated bullying, received a crash course in social media, and seen how easy it is for children to purposefully or accidently access pornographic websites. What you do now is up to you.

REALITY CHECK

HOW SAFE IS YOUR HOME?

1. When was the last time you spoke to your kids about the dangers of pornography?

2. Do you have a filter? How safe and effective is that filter?

3. What else can you do to make technology your friend and not your foe?

LEARN THE LINGO

I was watching the NBA Finals with my teenage nephew, who kept saying, "That is so wet" whenever a player took a shot. I kept thinking, "What is wet about a basketball shot? I know the players are sweaty, but the ball in the air?" I didn't get it. After about the tenth time he said it, I finally asked him what on earth he meant by that phrase. With a look of disgust that his ancient uncle didn't know, he explained that a good shot, one that was likely to go into the basket, is wet. As in, "it's raining basketballs." Still very abstract, but at least I now understand what the "in" crowd means when they yell "That is so wet" at a basketball game.

While this phrase has probably already been labeled as "so last year" and is no longer in circulation, the principle remains the same: parents, you should learn the latest, hippest lingo, not so you can speak it (that's just annoying), but so that you can understand what your children and their friends are saying. Think of this as learning a new dialect, one that has similarities to **TXTSPK** (text speak) but is not made up of acronyms and smiley faces.

But like trying to learn any new language, this task is not as easy as you may think, and may actually be harder. For example, in Afrikaans (the Dutch dialect spoken in South Africa where I grew up) there is pretty much one word for cool—*Lekker*! But kids have dozens. Some of the following words and phrases you may recognize, and some may be completely foreign to you. Some of these words only surfers should use and some are *not* cool ways of saying "cool" anymore. Are you lost yet? Let's see if you recognize the various iterations of "cool" (in alphabetical order).

Awesome, bodacious, chill, funky, cowabunga, dope, excellent, far out, groovy, hang ten, incredible, jumping Jehosophat, killer, laid back, ludicrous, mondo, gnarly, neat, nifty, off the chain, ostentatious, poundtastic, radical, sick, spectacular, tight, tubular, unbelievable, vicious, whack, wicked, zoolander.

As for what you *should* say without looking like a Neanderthal parent, I would recommend sticking with "cool" and leave the new vernacular to your children. "Cool" is ageless, never goes out of style, and is perfect in its simplicity.

Then, to complicate matters, words don't always mean what you think they mean. For example, "bad," "sick," and "wicked" all mean "good" (to teens), even though when used in their proper contexts they all mean bad things. Let me break it down for you:

Good: "I can't believe your mother bought you the new Xbox. That's *sick*."

Bad: "Dude, you stink. Are you *sick*?"

I don't expect any parent to truly master the lingo, unless that parent is a high school teacher and spend their days actually listening to, and talking with the natives. But awareness of our ignorance is a good place to start.

IF YOU LISTEN, THEY WILL TALK

For my day job, I get to do some fun things. Like the time I helped produce a training video based on generation gaps in the workplace. The type of video we were filming is what we call a "man in the street" video, which means the video is shot in public places, like busy streets, and with seemingly random people in those settings.

Spoiler alert: Reality programming and videos that have the opinions and comments of "complete strangers" on a street usually have actors playing the strangers. Yes, actors, with an agent, script, teleprompter, makeup, microphones, and lighting.

Although we used actors, microphones, and lighting, and started with a rough script, we still asked the actors (who were true representatives of their respective generations) what they thought of other generations. What we heard not only surprised us, but it also ended up on the final video.

Every person, regardless of age, said the same two phrases: "They just don't understand me." And "They just don't listen." We knew, based on the research and content we were filming for, that lack of understanding was a factor but not that it would be such a common theme.

In summary, our children do not think we understand them or listen to them. I realize this is not groundbreaking revelation for any of you reading this book, but it is the perceived reality of our children today. Just because we know something doesn't mean we are doing it very well. Like listening.

And this is one reality we must learn as parents: if you genuinely listen to your children, they will talk. And you want them to talk to you about everything.

Only if they feel listened to and not judged will they talk. If they don't talk to you, it will be with someone else, and you hope that someone has their best interests in mind. However, you are the best person for that job, so own it.

PERIODS HAPPEN

If you have daughters, this is the *other* talk that needs to happen sooner rather than later. Guess what? This talk can be a lot more stressful to talk about than the sex talk, probably because it's usually imminent and not off in the distant future.

For obvious reasons, this dialogue should ideally occur between a mother and daughter. As a father of four daughters, I want nothing to do with this talk. After all, what do I really know about what they're experiencing? This discussion is best held between a mother and daughter (or grandmother, aunt, or lady friend if mom isn't around).

After listening to my wife and reading what other women have said about this talk, though, I know that this talk can really be uncomfortable. Since every girl is different, there isn't one right approach either. Some girls just need to know the basics, while others want to know every detail of what is going to happen. When? Why? How long? And how they are supposed to know when it is going to happen? To give you an idea of how perplexing this concept is for a young girl, take a look at some actual questions asked by one in regards to tampons:

"What is that thing made out of, metal?"

"How far does it stick out of your body?"

"How long is it?"

"How do you get it out?"

"Are you serious? You have to pull a string?"

And these questions don't even represent a fraction of all the questions that can come up in regards to the blood, cramps, potential mood swings, and many other wonderful side effects associated with having a period.

Like the sex talk, the most important reality to remember is to have "the talk" *before* it's too late and they are traumatized for life. Since the beginning of time, women have been menstruating, but it's still a new experience for each girl and should not be a surprise. Discovering that you are bleeding and not knowing why would frighten anyone.

A friend recommended this great American Girl book to help teach daughters what they need to know about periods, and their changing bodies in general, in a safe and respectful way: *The Care and Keeping of You: The Body Book for Girls.*[18]

PREPARING FOR PERIODS

1. When should I talk with my daughter?

2. Do I know all the correct answers to all the potential questions?

3. If not, how do I plan to get prepared for "the talk" myself? By when?

THE TEENAGER AGREEMENT

As we have just read, children can be challenging sometimes, especially during their teenage years. With sassiness, dissent, disobedience, and outright rebellion, any time you can get agreement is a good time. Agreement can bring peace and stability to an otherwise volatile situation.

In this section, I'm suggesting that before you find yourself in a disagreeable situation, you and your teenage child should establish some ground rules by having a two-way dialogue on what is and what is not acceptable behavior for both parent and child. I know this sounds idealistic and that parenthood is realistic (as I've been promoting throughout the book), but with both parties proactively working on an agreement, I can promise you a more civil experience.

Think of looking for agreement as having "reality" talks with your teenage children on specific topics and then agreeing on what can and should be done when things get hard. It is not necessarily a contract because when emotions are involved, as they will be, forcing a stiff contract on someone you love usually doesn't work. It's just an agreement that both sides have figuratively signed off on—a safe place to return to when necessary.

These talks would ideally take place when your child is a pre-teen or young teen, while he or she is still pliable and impressionable. However, if positioned correctly and positively, these talks can take place during or after a disagreement with the intent to get both sides on the same page.

Reality Talk Topics

Below are thirteen reality talks every parent should have with their teenager. Note that the topics are broad. Please add your own angle or parenting paradigm (beliefs, values, and perspectives) to them.

1. Self-esteem
2. Our home and other people's homes
3. School and extracurricular activities
4. Money
5. Friends
6. Dating
7. Sex
8. College
9. Drugs, alcohol, and addictions
10. Diet and physical activity
11. TV, games, texting, and social media
12. Depression
13. Religion and spirituality

The Anatomy of a Reality Talk

Regardless of the topic, every reality talk can be broken down into the following pieces. Keep in mind that this is not an interrogation and that these steps are purely a suggested process, not a script to be followed verbatim. Use what you want in the way you want to. It's up to you how you do it. "The talk" itself does not have to be as formal as outlined below. On the contrary, it can be as simple as an informal talk with your teen on any subject that results in both of you coming away with a clear understanding and agreement on that subject.

1. **Share your intent candidly.** Talk plainly and honestly about your motivation for wanting to have the conversation and why you feel it important to come to agreement on that specific topic. For example, one way you could start any of the reality talks is by saying, "I know this may seem a little awkward, talking about [insert topic] with your father [or mother], but I feel it is important that we all come to an understanding and agreement on what is and is not acceptable. I first want to really listen to your thoughts and feelings around this subject. I want you to feel like I completely understand your point of view, and then I hope you will allow me to talk about my thoughts and feelings about the subject. This way we can both walk away from this talk being in complete agreement. Is that all right with you?"

2. **Ask your teen what he or she knows, feels, and thinks about the topic**.

3. **Listen intently to his or her answer from his or her point of view.** Restate and continue questioning so that you get past the superficial answers and down to what he

or she really feel. **FYI** (for your information), you will get a lot of shallow answers with the intent to test your real intent to understand, so always dig deeper.

4. **Talk about the *consequences* and *rewards* for breaking the agreement or living up to it.** Be real. Talk about real-life consequences and rewards, not just the results in your family life. For example, a mother took her young teenage daughter to meet with a family friend who had gotten pregnant when she was a teenager. They talked about everything candidly: why she had sex with the boy at the time, how he reacted when she became pregnant, and the difficult choices she had to make on her own, including whether to keep the child or give him up for adoption. She also explained the emotional stress, the social ramifications, and how that one decision to sleep with a boy ultimately affected her whole life. You can imagine how effective this talk was in teaching the realities surrounding just one of those topics.

5. **Find sincere agreement.** Do not push your agenda or expectations on your child. For these talks to truly work, your child must feel understood and respected.

6. **Establish some ground rules.** While these talks should be informal and natural, it would also be beneficial to establish some fundamental ground rules. For starters, stay connected and accountable to one another. Decide how often you two should touch base on life in general and on this agreement in particular. Should it be done informally or more formally with a scheduled calendar event? Who will initiate the discussion?

Allow for agreement addenda. Opinions change, perspectives grow, interests evolve, and personalities mature. Be flexible and open to changes to agreement as long as you talk about it together and agree upon what the changes are.

Together you should decide whether you want to write down what you agree upon or have more of an informal approach. In my opinion (**IMO**), writing it down is always a better option as it makes the *what* absolutely clear and not open for interpretation.

REALITY CHECK

WHICH OF THESE TALKS HAVE YOU HAD WITH YOUR TEEN?

- ☐ Self-esteem
- ☐ Our home other peoples home's
- ☐ School and additional activities
- ☐ Money
- ☐ Friends
- ☐ Dating
- ☐ Sex
- ☐ College
- ☐ Drugs, alcohol, addictions
- ☐ Diet and physical activity
- ☐ TV, games, texting, and social media
- ☐ Depression
- ☐ Religion and spirituality

If not, when? Schedule some one-on-one time now.

NOTES

1. American Psychiatric Association (APA) 2010 Annual Meeting, May 24, 2010, poster abstract NR3-12; Anderson et al., "Violent Video Game Effects on Aggression, Empathy, and Prosocial Behavior in Eastern and Western Countries." *Psychological Bulletin* no. 136 (2010), 151–173.

2. "Some Children Really Are Addicted to Video Games," last modified April 20, 2009, http://www.livescience.com/health/090420-children-video-games-addicted.html.

3. "Media and Children," The American Academy of Pediatrics, last modified January 23, 2014, http://www.aap.org/en-us/advocacy-and-policy/aap-health-initiatives/pages/media-and-children.aspx.

4. "ESRB Ratings Guide," Entertainment Software Rating Board, last modified January 23, 2014, http://www.esrb.org/ratings/ratings_guide.jsp.

5. Victoria J. Rideout, Ulla G. Foehr, and Donald F. Roberts, *Generation M²: Media in the Lives of 8- to 18-Year-Olds* (Menlo Park, CA: The Henry J. Kaiser Family Foundation, 2010), http://kaiserfamilyfoundation.files.wordpress.com/2013/01/8010.pdf.

6. Joaquin Phoenix and Michael Honda, "Column: Our Children Face a Bullying Epidemic," *USA Today* online, August 28, 2012, http://usatoday30.usatoday.com/news/opinion/forum/story/2012-08-28/joaquin-phoenix-bullying-epidemic/57379318/1.

7. "Bullying Definition," accessed January 24, 2014, http://www.stopbullying.gov/what-is-bullying/index.html.

8. S. Hinduja and J. W. Patchin, *Bullying Beyond the Schoolyard: Preventing and Responding to Cyberbullying* (Thousand Oaks, CA: Sage Publications, 2009).

9. "Teen Suicide Statistics," HealthyChildren.org, http://www.healthychildren.org/English/health-issues/conditions/emotional-problems/pages/Teen-Suicide-Statistics.aspx; "CDC: Teen suicide attempts on the rise." FoxNews.com, http://www.foxnews.com/health/2012/06/08/cdc-teen-suicide-attempts-on-rise/

10. Pew Research Center's Internet and American Life Project, "Social Media and Young Adults," February 3, 2010, accessed November 2011, www.pewresearch.org/pubs/1484/social-media-mobile-internet-use-teens-millennials-fewer-blog.

11. Victoria J. Rideout, Ulla G. Foehr, and Donald F. Roberts, *Generation M²: Media in the Lives of 8- to 18-Year-Olds* (Menlo Park, CA: The Henry J. Kaiser Family Foundation, 2010), http://kaiserfamilyfoundation.files.wordpress.com/2013/01/8010.pdf.

12.   Video Game Addiction, "Symptoms of Video Game Addiction in Teens," http://www.video-game-addiction.org/symptoms-computer-addiction-teens.html.

13.   Jerry Ropelato, "Tricks Pornographers Play," accessed January 24, 2014, http://internet-filter-review.toptenreviews.com/tricks-pornographers-play.html.

14.   Jochen Peter and Patti M. Valkenburg, "Adolescents' Exposure to Sexually Explicit Internet Material, Sexual Uncertainty, and Attitudes Toward Uncommitted Sexual Exploration: Is There a Link?" *Communication Research* 35, no. 5 (2008): 579–601.

15.   Anita Chandra, Steven C. Martino, Rebecca L. Collins, Marc N. Elliott, Sandra H. Berry, David E. Kanouse, and Angela Miu, "Does Watching Sex on Television Predict Teen Pregnancy? Findings from a Longitudinal Survey of Youth," *Pediatrics* 122 (2008): 1047–1054.

16.   Peter and Valkenburg, "Adolescents' Exposure to Sexually Explicit Internet Material," 579–601.

17.   Michele L. Ybarra and Kimberly J. Mitchell, "Exposure to Internet Pornography among Children and Adolescents: A National Survey," *CyberPsychology & Behavior* 8 (2005). Vincent Cyrus Yoder, Thomas B.Virden III, and Kiran Amin "Internet Pornography and Loneliness: An Association?" *Sexual Addiction & Compulsivity* 12 (2005).

18.   Valorie Schafer, *The Care and Keeping of You: The Body Book for Girls*, (Middleton, WI: Pleasant Company Publications, American Girl, LLC, 1998).

TXTSPK FINAL EXAMINATION

AS YOU HAVE PROBABLY DISCOVERED BY READING this book, once you crack the acronym and emoticon code, txtspk is pretty easy to understand. And understanding should be your goal, because there a lot of texting is going on. In fact, American teens are texting all the time—on average they're sending or receiving 3,339 texts a month. That's more than six per every hour they're awake.[1]

So after reading the whole book, how well do you know your txtspk? Try to fill in as many of the blanks on the following questionnaire as possible. (If you need to cheat, the answers can be found on the **TXTSPK** summary pages that follow the questionnaire).

TY:

A2D:

BTW:

F2F:

FB:

FWIW:

FYI:

IMHO:

IMO:

IRL:

IU2U:

JSYK:

MNC: TBD:
NOOB: TMI:
OH: WTH:
OMG: YW:
PAW: XOXO:
PLS OR PLZ:
ROFL: And hundreds of other acro-
SRSLY: nyms and emoticons added
                daily…

TXTSPK SUMMARY AND ANSWER KEY

TY: Thank you

A2D: Agree to disagree

BTW: By the way

F2F or FTF: Face to face

FB: Facebook

FWIW: For what it's worth

FYI: For your information

IMHO: In my honest opinion/
   In my humble opinion

IMO: In my opinion

IRL: In real life

IU2U: It's up to you

JSYK: Just so you know

MNC: Mother nature calls

NOOB: Newcomer, Rookie,
   Amateur

OH: Overheard

OMG: Oh my gosh!

PAW: Parents are watching

PLS or PLZ: Please

ROFL: Rolling on the floor
laughing

SRSLY: Seriously

TBD: To be determined

TMI: too much information

WTH: What the heck?

YW: Your'e welcome

XOXO: hugs and kisses

And hundreds of other acronyms and emoticons added
daily . . .

NOTE

1. "U.S. Teen Mobile Report: Calling Yesterday, Texting Today, Using Apps Tomorrow," The Nielsen Company (October 2010), http://www.nielsen.com/us/en/newswire/2010/u-s-teen-mobile-report-calling-yesterday-texting-today-using-apps-tomorrow.html.

ABOUT THE AUTHOR

TREION MOVED TO THE UNITED STATES FROM South Africa in 1995 to attend college, where he graduated with honors and married the most beautiful woman in the world. After working for a time in the "real world," he continued his studies and received a master's degree in adult learning, which he uses daily as FranklinCovey's Director of Development for the Online Learning and Digital Solutions Group.

In addition to authoring parenting books, Treion is also a business book author, national presenter, and social media and online learning expert. Treion also draws inspiration from his experiences as a professional dancer, medic in the South African Army, missionary, university student body president, university mascot (the Thunderbird), and professional speaker.

Treion is also the author of *Dad Rules: A Simple Manual for a Complex Job, Mom Rules: Because Even Superheroes Need Help Sometimes* (coauthored with his wife, Soni), *The Learning Explosion*, and *The Webinar Manifesto*.

STAY CONNECTED WITH TREION

Website: Rules4Families.com
Blog: The Booger Blog
Facebook: Rules4Families

Twitter: @Treeon
LinkedIn: treionmuller
Pinterest: treion

Thank you for buying my book! I'd love it if you would leave a review on Amazon. Feedback helps make future versions and books better.

—Treion

DAD RULES

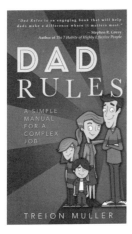

Kids don't come with a manual and so far there's no app for fatherhood, but that doesn't mean you should parent empty-handed. No matter what fathering challenges you face, you can find the answer in here—along with a healthy dose of humor. Whether you're a dad to tots or teens, these simple but effective dad rules are guaranteed to get the job done right.

MOM RULES

While it is universally understood that being a mother takes superhuman patience, strength, and fortitude, even these everyday superheroes need a helping hand every once in a while. *Mom Rules* is a quick go-to guide of essential rules to help mothers know what to expect, what to say, and what to do in those difficult moments when they are at their wit's end.

0 26575 13972 3